THE PHOTOSHOP® CS2 SPEED CLINIC

AUTOMATING PHOTOSHOP TO GET TWICE THE WORK DONE IN HALF THE TIME

MATT KLOSKOWSKI

EDUCATION AND CURRICULUM DEVELOPER
NATIONAL ASSOCIATION OF PHOTOSHOP PROFESSIONALS

**The Photoshop® CS2
Speed Clinic Team**

CREATIVE DIRECTOR
Felix Nelson

TECHNICAL EDITORS
**Kim Doty
Cindy Snyder**

PRODUCTION EDITOR
Kim Gabriel

PRODUCTION MANAGER
Dave Damstra

COVER DESIGN AND
CREATIVE CONCEPTS
Jessica Maldonado

COVER PHOTOS
COURTESY OF
iStockphoto.com

PUBLISHED BY
Peachpit Press

Copyright © 2006 by Kelby Books, LLC

FIRST EDITION: March 2006

Composed in *ITC Franklin Gothic* (International Typeface Corporation), *ITC Blair* (ITC) and *Bullet* (House Industries) by NAPP Publishing.

Trademarks
All terms mentioned in this book that are known to be trademarks or service marks have been appropriately capitalized. Peachpit Press cannot attest to the accuracy of this information. Use of a term in the book should not be regarded as affecting the validity of any trademark or service mark.

Macintosh is a registered trademark of Apple Computer.
Windows is a registered trademark of Microsoft Corporation.
Photoshop is a registered trademark of Adobe Systems Incorporated.

Warning and Disclaimer
This book is designed to provide information about Photoshop CS2 tips. Every effort has been made to make this book as complete and as accurate as possible, but no warranty of fitness is implied.

The information is provided on an as-is basis. The author and Peachpit Press shall have neither liability nor responsibility to any person or entity with respect to any loss or damages arising from the information contained in this book or from the use of the discs or programs that may accompany it.

ISBN 0-321-44165-6

9 8 7 6 5 4 3 2 1

Printed and bound in the United States of America

www.peachpit.com
www.scottkelbybooks.com

*For my wife, Diana, and
my two boys, Ryan and Justin.
You guys are hands down
the best things that
ever happened to me.*

ACKNOWLEDGMENTS

First, I'd like to thank one of the most important people in my life—my incredibly beautiful, funny, caring, sensitive, and fun-loving wife, Diana. I have the easy job. I get to go to work every day to do what I love and get paid for it. She works 10 times as hard as I do and never seems to wear down. I'll always be grateful for the wonderful job you do raising our kids each day while still managing to have an ear-to-ear smile on your face when I come home. You're the best wife a guy could hope for.

Next, I owe more thanks than they'll ever know to my two sons, Ryan and Justin. The two of you put things into perspective for me in ways that you'll never be aware of and just make me the absolute proudest dad I could have ever hoped to be. No matter how much I work, what I write, or whatever I do, my favorite thing in the world is still our weekly "Guys Night Out." Granted, it consists of mini-golf, video games, and ice cream but I wouldn't trade that time together with my buddies for all of the book deals in the world.

None of this would be worth anything without people to share it with and I'm lucky enough to have the best family a guy could hope for. First, thanks go to my mom and dad for giving me such a great start. I'd also like to thank my brother and sister and their spouses, Ed, Kerry, Kristine, and Scott. You've all been such a positive influence in my life and your support means the world to me.

I'd also like to thank Scott Kelby. One day I got a call from Barbie Taylor (KW Media Group's Human Resources Director, and so much more). She asked me to come in to talk to Scott about a permanent position with the National Association of Photoshop Professionals. That day changed my career and my life and I owe a great debt to Scott. All I can say is thank you. You've not only given me tremendous opportunities, but you've become a great friend and role model of mine in the process and I'm honestly not sure which to be more thankful for.

To Dave Moser, I'd like to say that I will not be the fish on your wall (weird inside joke that only he will get). Seriously, your constant pushing (to say the least) is what makes this book and everything else I do even better and better. Thanks for always reminding me to strive to be better, but more importantly thanks for becoming a great buddy as well.

I'd also like to thank Dave Cross. I say this over and over again in every book I've written since I've known him but I feel compelled to continue to say that Dave is a 100% class act in this industry. If there is any person to follow personally, professionally, and ethically, Dave is the one.

Special thanks go to Felix Nelson, Dave Damstra, and Jessica Maldonado. The book you're holding in your hands looks as great as it does only because of them and their amazing ideas. Trust me, if you had seen the raw material handed in for this book, you would have no doubt why these guys are the best in the industry. Many thanks also go to Kim Gabriel for keeping this project, as well as the million (okay, maybe it's only 50, but it's still a lot) other projects we do, going at the same time.

I also don't know what I would have done without our two tech and copy editors, Cindy Snyder and Kim Doty. The two of you are editing machines and you do it all with a smile on your face (and I know I'm not that funny). I'll never forget the day Cindy asked me, "How can you manage to capitalize Camera Raw four different ways in the same paragraph?!" I can only imagine how hard it is to do what you do and I truly appreciate all of your hard work to make this book the best.

Many thanks also go to Scott Cowlin, Nancy Ruenzel, Rachel Tiley, and Ted Waitt at Peachpit for continuing to be leaders in this industry and giving me the opportunity to do what I love to do.

I'd also like to thank some of my friends at Adobe. Namely, Julieanne Kost, Terry White, Russell Brown, Jeff Tranberry, Marc Pawliger, and Tom Ruark. Your input and insights into Photoshop have helped me tremendously.

Finally, I owe a special debt of gratitude to you, the reader. I truly appreciate being able to write books and I appreciate you taking your time to read this one. You are the reason why this book is here in the first place. The constant feedback and encouragement I get from people in the form of website feedback, phone calls, emails, and introductions at conferences is what makes this the most fun for me. Thank you.

ABOUT THE AUTHOR

Matt Kloskowski is the Education and Curriculum Developer for the National Association of Photoshop Professionals, and is a speaker at trade shows and events around the world. He's a co-host of the top-rated video podcast *Photoshop TV*, and has written four books on Photoshop and Illustrator, including *Photoshop CS2 Savvy* and *Illustrator CS2 Killer Tips*. Matt is featured on various training DVDs available from www.photoshopvideos.com and is a regular writer for *Photoshop User* magazine, *Layers* magazine, and the *Photoshop Elements Techniques* newsletter. He's an instructor at Photoshop World and the MacLive Conference, and teaches basic and advanced Photoshop classes for Sessions.edu Online School of Design. Matt is also an Adobe Certified Expert in Photoshop, as well as a Macromedia Flash Certified Developer.

MATT KLOSKOWSKI

TABLE OF CONTENTS

TABLE OF CONTENTS

TABLE OF CONTENTS

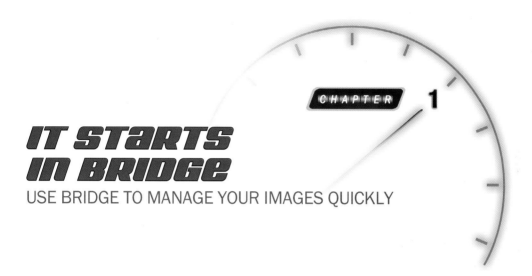

CHAPTER 1

IT STARTS IN BRIDGE

USE BRIDGE TO MANAGE YOUR IMAGES QUICKLY

It really all does start out in Bridge. I mean, there are a ton of ways to do things faster in Photoshop, but what better way to really begin to work faster than by learning how to find, protect, get to, and organize your images the right way in the first place? Adobe Bridge is exactly the place to start doing this. Do me a favor, though. If you're used to the File Browser in previous versions of Photoshop, make sure you still read this chapter because Bridge is not just File Browser with a facelift. It's a totally new beast by itself and has some incredible timesaving features available inside it. Plus, the very first tutorial in this chapter gives you some vital info about how to read this book and where to access the download files if you want to follow along.

HOW TO READ THIS BOOK

At the beginning of every tutorial in this book, you'll find a little story. My favorite teachers and instructors throughout the years taught me in a way I wasn't aware of then—they told stories. It didn't matter if the stories were true or fake because they got the point across and did it well. So, that's the direction in which I've taken this book. Each tutorial comes from an actual story that happened to me or someone I know. That's how I know this stuff works in the real world because each and every part of this book came from people who actually use Photoshop and wanted to get something done faster.

STEP ONE:

This part is where I'll explain step-by-step what to do. Keep in mind, though, I'm assuming that if you bought a book on doing things faster in Photoshop that you already know the basics of using Photoshop. I'll do my best to make things as clear as possible but I won't be explaining things you already know, such as how to open and close images, what a layer is, or how to use many of the tools in the Toolbox. Don't mind the photo here on the right. I just take any opportunity I can to work my two sons into my books.

©MATT KLOSKOWSKI

There are small places in between steps that'll look just like this one does. You'll be able to recognize them because of the small icon next to them. These are areas that may trip you up or slow you down. I'll try to warn you about any little nuances or things that could keep you from working faster.

TURBO BOOST

This is one of those speed tips I talk about in Step Two. Trust me, you'll want to read these on every page. Sometimes they relate to the tutorial on that page but sometimes they're just fast ways to do something.

STEP TWO:

Make sure you read the small gems at the bottom corner of each page called "Turbo Boost." They're not just there because I had to fill up the space. Trust me, the editors and designers that worked on this book would have loved it if I tossed this idea, but I think it's an essential part of the book. Plus, it's the only way I could fit in all of the little speed-related tips I wanted you to know. These are 100% speed-related tips, workarounds, shortcuts, or tricks that will help you be more productive.

STEP THREE:

Oh yeah, most of the time you'll see an image next to each step to help illustrate what we're covering (or to just make things look pretty). You can try to skip reading the text and just look at the image but you're probably better off looking at both. Again, disregard this image, as I'm just building brownie points with my beautiful wife Diana.

STEP FOUR:

Where appropriate, I've provided the photos and the images I'm using in this book on a website for you to download. If it's a Bridge tutorial, well, you can figure out that you don't need to have the same images in Bridge that I do. However, if it's a tutorial that uses a photo or image with specific layers, then I went ahead and included it at www.scottkelbybooks .com/speedclinic for download.

TURBO BOOST

Here's another one of those speed tips. The tip here is to not read the rest of this one. This is the only one that you'll find that just fills space because I needed to fill space in this introduction. Read the rest of them, though!

CREATING YOUR OWN BRIDGE WORKSPACE

When I first saw Bridge I thought, "This is just a facelift of the File Browser." Once I really started using it my thoughts quickly changed to "This rocks!" One thing I found myself doing a lot was moving and resizing all of the panels to suit my needs at the moment. When I first downloaded photos onto my computer, I wanted Bridge to have one view while I reviewed them, and then when I was going through trying to pick my favorites, I wanted another view. That's where workspaces come in. They're easy to create and they help speed things up when you're working in Bridge.

STEP ONE:

First, let's all start from the same place. Launch Bridge from Photoshop by choosing File>Browse, pressing Command-Option-O (PC: Control-Alt-O), or clicking the Go to Bridge button on the Options Bar. You can also launch Bridge without even having Photoshop open. Once you're in Bridge, if the Favorites palette is open (at the top of the Panel area to the left), choose View>Favorites Panel to remove the checkmark and close it.

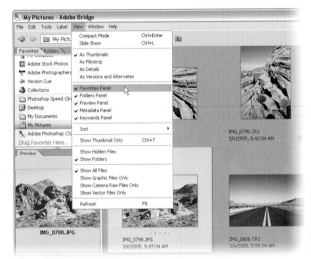

STEP TWO:

Do the same and close all other palettes with a checkmark next to them, except for the Preview palette. This will now only leave your thumbnail preview in the main Bridge window and in the Preview palette on the left.

TURBO BOOST

There are some keyboard shortcuts that are just plain too hard to memorize. However, the workspace shortcuts are definitely worth it. Plus, they're pretty easy. Just remember that they all involve the Command key (PC: Control key) and an F1 through F5 key, depending on which workspace you want.

IMG_0798.JPG

STEP THREE:
Now, expand your Preview palette so it takes up nearly the entire screen. Also, decrease the size of the thumbnails to make them smaller by sliding the Thumbnail Size slider (near the bottom right of the Bridge window) to the left. We're only trying to concentrate on getting the largest preview possible right now.

STEP FOUR:
Once you're happy with the way this view looks, choose Window>Workspace>Save Workspace. Enter "Large Preview" in the Name field. Make sure the Save Window Location as Part of Workspace checkbox is turned on to save the exact location of this Bridge window on your screen. Note that you can assign a keyboard shortcut, too.

TURBO BOOST

You can use Bridge for more than just looking at images. If you click on a PDF file, you'll see that you can page through the PDF in the Preview palette.

STEP FIVE:

When you're done, click Save and this workspace will be saved. Now you can always change over to this saved workspace by choosing it from Window>Workspace. (*Note:* Your saved workspaces will appear at the bottom of the menu.)

Don't try to rearrange your palettes each time you want to get back to Bridge defaults. To get back to the default workspace as it was when you first installed Bridge, just choose Window>Workspace> Reset to Default Workspace or press Command-F1 (PC: Control-F1) and you're back to normal.

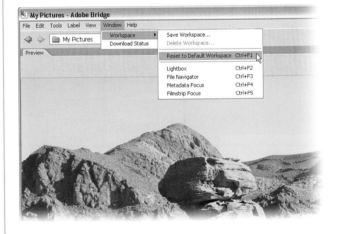

TURBO BOOST

You can actually play movie files (WMV, AVI, QuickTime, etc.) inside Bridge. Just click on the file and you'll see the play controls appear in the Preview pane. Click Play, and the movie, sound and everything, will start playing.

©MATT KLOSKOWSKI

What if I told you a story about how much I love adding or changing the file info (aka metadata) on my photos and images? You'd think I was a liar and you'd be right on. However, when I first started working with the file info for each image, I quickly thought to myself that there's got to be a better way (and there is).

CHANGING THE FILE INFO (METADATA) ON MULTIPLE IMAGES

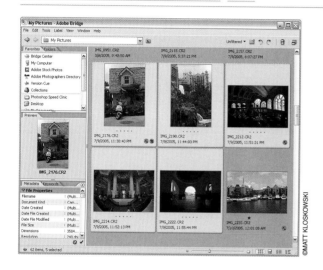

©MATT KLOSKOWSKI

©MATT KLOSKOWSKI

STEP ONE:

In Bridge, navigate until you see a group of images for which you'd like to change the file info. Select one of the photo thumbnails and then press-and-hold the Command (PC: Control) key and click to select multiple images.

STEP TWO:

Look in the Metadata palette at the bottom of the Panel area. You'll see File Properties at the top of the palette, but you won't be able to change any of these items. Right below that you'll see IPTC Core, and below that you'll see Camera Data (EXIF). You can change the IPTC Core data, but not the Camera Data. So, click once on the Creator item at the top of the IPTC Core section. You will receive a warning dialog alerting you that you're about to edit the information on multiple photos. Click Yes to dismiss this warning.

TURBO BOOST

If you're the organized type, then you may want to see your file info in a categorized way. Instead of using the Metadata palette, you can always select the photos you'd like to change, choose File>File Info, and add your information in the resulting dialog. For me, the palette is just faster to access and it lets me stay in the same view where I can see all of my photos.

Don't bother trying to edit data that is not editable. You'll know which data you can edit because it'll have a little pencil icon next to it. No pencil means no changing.

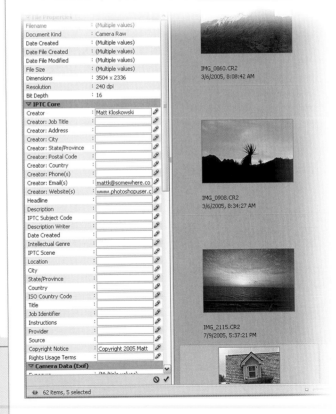

STEP THREE:

You'll see that all of the editable fields now turn into small text boxes. Go ahead and enter the information that is needed for your images. In this example, I've entered my name in the Creator field, as well as my email and website addresses in those fields. I've also entered in the Copyright Notice field, "Copyright 2005 Matt Kloskowski."

TURBO BOOST

Want to see your photos on a black background in Bridge? Just go to Bridge's General Preferences and move the Background slider all the way to the left (toward Black).

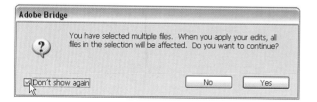

STEP FOUR:

Click outside of the Metadata palette to save your settings (or just click the Apply checkmark at the bottom of the palette). When you click outside of the palette, you will receive a warning dialog asking if you want to apply the metadata changes to the selected files. Just click Apply. Now the text boxes will be gone and your metadata fields will reflect the information entered.

 The warning dialogs that keep popping up can get annoying. When they pop up for the first time, feel free to turn on the Don't Show Again checkbox if you feel comfortable not seeing them every time you try to make a change. Trust me, it's a little thing that will save you a ton of time.

TURBO BOOST

You can show or hide the details under each thumbnail in Bridge by pressing Command-T (PC: Control-T).

USING METADATA TEMPLATES TO CHANGE FILE INFO ON MULTIPLE IMAGES

The previous tutorial worked great for me when I had very specific file info for groups of images in a single project, but that file info may change for each project. One thing I noticed, though, was that many times I had standard file info (such as website and copyright info) that didn't change from project to project. You don't have to re-enter that info every time because there is something called a metadata template. Type it once and Photoshop can remember it for you and apply it to other groups of images as well.

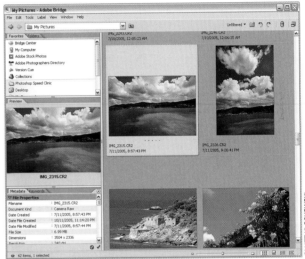

@MATT KLOSKOWSKI

STEP ONE:

For this example, you'll need to start with a photo to base your template on. So, go ahead and find a photo in Bridge, and click once on the thumbnail to select it.

STEP TWO:

From Bridge's menu bar, choose File>File Info and you'll get a large dialog with a lot of intimidating text boxes. On the left side of the dialog is a list of metadata categories and on the right are the accompanying items for each of those categories. Don't worry about entering info for all of the fields, just type in something for the Author, Copyright Notice, and Copyright Info URL fields. Don't click OK yet, because we're not done.

TURBO BOOST

You can set Bridge to automatically launch when you start Photoshop by opening the General Preferences dialog in Photoshop and turning on the Automatically Launch Bridge checkbox in the Options section.

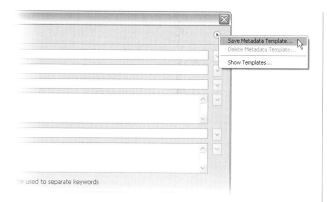

©MATT KLOSKOWSKI

STEP THREE:
After typing in your info, look in the top-right corner of the dialog. There's a small, right-facing triangle there just begging to be clicked. So give in and click it, and select Save Metadata Template from the flyout menu.

STEP FOUR:
You'll get another small dialog asking you to name this template, so go ahead and enter a descriptive name, and click Save.

Don't just name your template "Template 1" (you know you're guilty of naming things Template 1, Template 2, Template 3, and so on). Doing that really slows you down and makes it hard to remember what that template is when you're looking at this two weeks later, especially if you've created more than one template.

STEP FIVE:
Okay, now that you've created the template you never need to re-enter that information again, but you'll need to know how to use it. Just click Cancel to close the file info dialog (you don't even need to save the settings for this file, if you don't want to). Then select an image in Bridge that you'd like to apply the template to. Press-and-hold the Command (PC: Control) key and select any other images that you'd also like to add the same info to.

 *TURBO BOOST*

Press Command-Shift-I (PC: Control-Shift-I) to select every image but the currently selected image in Bridge.

STEP SIX:

Go to the Metadata palette and click the small, right-facing triangle at the top right to display the palette's flyout menu. Choose Append Metadata, and then choose the template that you just saved.

STEP SEVEN:

A warning dialog will appear asking if you're sure you want to apply this file info to multiple files. I suggest you turn on the Don't Show Again checkbox and then click Yes. Bridge will apply the same metadata template to all of your selected photos. Pretty simple, huh? Just click on one of the photos and you can see that its metadata has been changed in the Metadata palette.

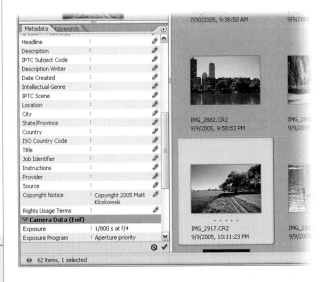

TURBO BOOST

Quickly increase or decrease the thumbnail preview size in Bridge by pressing the same keyboard shortcuts you would use in Photoshop—Command–+ (PC: Control–+) or Command–- (PC: Control–-).

I can't count how many times I was working on a project and my boss or client would come by and want to see what I had so far. It was such a pain to open files up in Photoshop just to show them off. This is where the Slide Show mode in Bridge really comes in handy. Now you can easily show off your images. It's also a great tool for reviewing your photos after a photo shoot. Not only do you get a huge preview of the photo, but you can also actually do things to them like rotate, rank, or delete them altogether.

CREATING A SLIDE SHOW

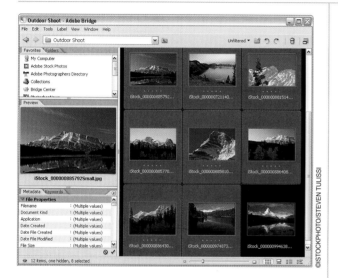

©ISTOCKPHOTO/STEVEN TULISSI

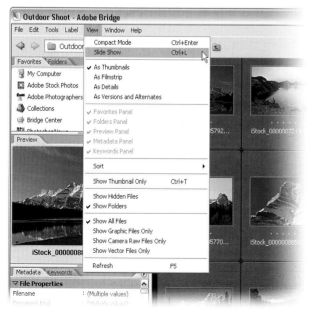

STEP ONE:
Open a folder in Bridge that contains the photos you'd like to see in a slide show.

Showing the entire folder of images in a slide show can take a while if you've got hundreds of images in it. If you don't want to show the entire folder, you can just as easily select the photos you do want to show by clicking on one and then pressing-and-holding the Command (PC: Control) key, and clicking on the others that you want to see.

STEP TWO:
After you've selected the photos you want to show in the slide show, just choose View>Slide Show. Now, I tend to use the keyboard shortcut here a lot, which is Command-L (PC: Control-L). Just imagine that it's a "lide show" instead of a slide show and that'll make it easier to remember.

TURBO BOOST

To deselect all selected images in Bridge, choose Edit>Deselect or press Command-Shift-A (PC: Control-Shift-A). I know, it's a little different from Photoshop but that's just the way it is.

STEP THREE:

Okay, now that you're in Slide Show mode, you can press the Spacebar to start the slide show. The slide show will automatically advance every few seconds (4 seconds by default). You can choose to wait or you can always use the arrow keys to advance to the next slide manually.

STEP FOUR:

While you're in Slide Show mode, there are a bunch of things that you can do to your photos. Just press the H key to show (or hide) a semi-opaque screen that displays the keyboard shortcuts for what's available. Finally, if you want to get out of Slide Show mode, just press the Escape key and that'll bring you back to Bridge.

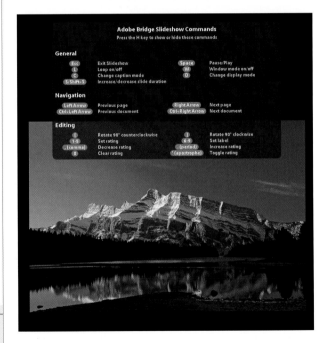

TURBO BOOST

In Slide Show mode, if you see a photo you want to open in Photoshop just press the O key.

Raise your hand if you like the way your camera names your photos. I can't see you, but I'm pretty sure there aren't any hands raised right now. Well, before Photoshop had the Batch Rename feature, renaming a few hundred photos could take some time. But with Batch Rename it's much easier. There's even a new feature in Photoshop CS2 that makes the process a lot more useful.

RENAMING MULTIPLE PHOTOS ALL AT ONCE

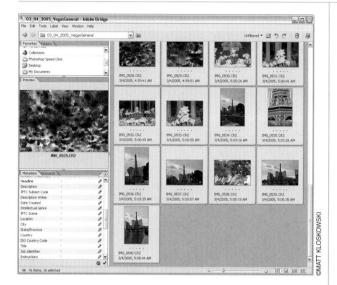

©MATT KLOSKOWSKI

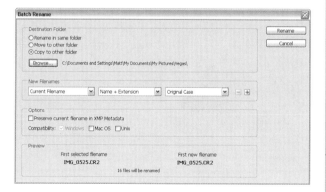

STEP ONE:
In Bridge, select the thumbnails of the images you want to rename. You can press Command-A (PC: Control-A) to Select All, or just press-and-hold the Command (PC: Control) key and click on individual images to rename only specific ones.

STEP TWO:
Once the images you want to rename are selected, choose Tools>Batch Rename or press Command-Shift-R (PC: Control-Shift-R). The Batch Rename dialog will appear with your renaming options. The Destination Folder section at the top of the dialog is an important one and has something new for CS2 users. Here, you need to choose where you want your renamed images to go. If you want them renamed in the same folder, then choose Rename in Same Folder. However, if you pick this option then all of your originals will be renamed. The next option, Move to Other Folder, renames your images and moves them to another folder. Finally, the last option, Copy to Other Folder, is my favorite (and is what's new in CS2). This one copies your images to another folder and renames them there. It leaves your original files untouched.

TURBO BOOST

You can always look at the Preview section at the bottom of the Batch Rename dialog to see what your new file name looks like. It shows you the original file name on the left, an example of the renamed file on the right, and lets you know exactly how many files will be renamed.

Many government agencies, as well as medical and forensic companies, require that the original file names be kept intact. If this affects you, then the best option here is usually Copy to Other Folder. This is mainly because it keeps your originals intact. It could prevent you from having to spend a ton of time later tracking down original file names.

STEP THREE:

The second section, New Filenames, deals with how you want to rename your images. It looks a little tricky, but once you get the hang of it you'll have a lot of options for your file names. The most popular choice from the first pop-up menu is Text. After you choose Text, you'll see a text field appear to the right of the menu. Type in some descriptive name here to help you remember what these photos are all about. I'll use "Vegas" since that's where these photos were taken.

STEP FOUR:

That's not it, though. If we just left it like this all of our photos would be named "Vegas" and that's not good. So, click on the small plus sign (+) icon all the way to the right. This will add another line of options for you. From the new pop-up menu on the left, choose Sequence Number. Then make sure to type the number 1 in the center text field. Finally, pick Two Digits from the pop-up menu on the right.

TURBO BOOST

You can toggle through Bridge's thumbnail views by pressing Command-\ (PC: Control-\) to switch between different modes.

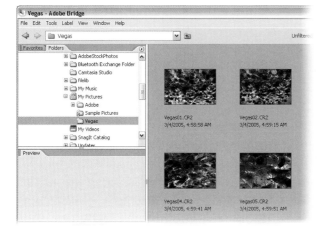

Make sure that you pick enough digits to cover the number of photos you have. Here, I picked Two Digits because I have less than 100 images in this folder. If you have more or you're not sure, then you may want to pick Three Digits or another appropriate number that will cover the number of images you have to rename. It'll save you a lot of time should Photoshop run into a problem because there are more images than you've allotted digits for.

STEP FIVE:

The third section in the dialog allows us to pick some options. It's best to turn on the Preserve Current Filename in XMP Metadata checkbox here. This makes sure that you always know what the original image was named in case you ever need it.

STEP SIX:

Now, click Rename and Batch Rename will work its magic. It may take a moment or two depending on how many images you have. When it's done, you may be able to see the results right in front of you. However, if you've chosen to copy the images to another folder (which I recommend), then you'll have to navigate Bridge to that folder to see the renamed images. (If you're choosing to copy the images to another folder, you will first need to click the Browse button in the Destination Folder section, and select a destination folder, before clicking Rename and running Batch Rename.)

TURBO BOOST

You can rotate your images directly in Bridge by pressing Command-[(PC: Control-[) or Command-] (PC: Control-]).

LETTING BRIDGE BUILD THE CACHE FOR YOU

After I'm done with a photo shoot, I usually can't wait to see what I've shot. So I proceed to connect my card reader and transfer my photos to my computer. After I do that, I fire up Bridge and start to review them, but that's where the process slows down. Bridge needs to build the thumbnails and cache for all of my photos, and if I shoot 200–300 photos that can take a while. That's where this feature comes in. I let Bridge do the cache building for me while I unpack my gear, and then when it's done I can review the photos with no interruptions.

WHAT IS CACHE?

First, let's get something cleared up. In Bridge, the cache is where all thumbnail, metadata, and general file information is stored. Bridge saves this cache to shorten the time it takes to preview photos in a folder. However, it does take time to create this cache (especially for RAW files). That's why it's best to follow this tutorial and have Bridge create the cache before you try to view your photos. That way they'll display a lot quicker when you're reviewing them.

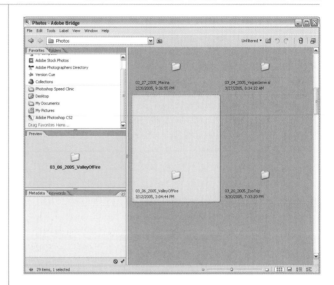

TURBO BOOST

If the large Bridge window gets in your way but you always want your photos close, just choose View>Compact Mode or press the Compact Mode button in the upper-right corner of Bridge's Options Bar.

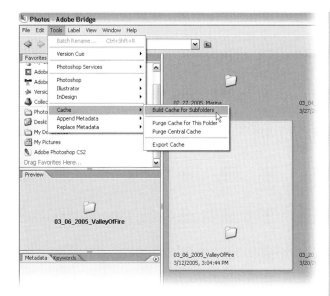

STEP ONE:

Once you've loaded all of your photos from the card reader onto your computer, navigate to the folder containing them in Bridge. From the Bridge menu, choose Tools>Cache>Build Cache for Subfolders.

STEP TWO:

After you choose this, you'll see a small dialog indicating that Bridge is building the cache for the photos and how many photos it has processed so far. Here's where you walk away and unpack your gear or go get that cup of coffee, as it'll take a few minutes. But when you get back, you're ready to roll and previewing your photos will be a much smoother process.

TURBO BOOST

When in Compact Mode, press the little button to the right of the Folder pop-up menu at the top of the Bridge window to switch to Ultra-Compact Mode. Now that's small, but you can quickly get to Bridge if you need it.

FASTER SEARCHING WITH KEYWORDS

After about the 58th time I found myself searching for photos, I was exasperated with the time I spent on searches. I kept thinking there has got to be a better way...and there is. Bridge contains a better way to search your images by adding keywords. This was especially useful for me since just grouping photos into folders wasn't enough. I needed a more fine-tuned way of finding images, and keywords are it.

STEP ONE:
Find some photos in Bridge that you want to add keywords to. For example, I recently went on a vacation with my family, so I've loaded those photos into Bridge.

STEP TWO:
Now, look over to the left side of the screen. Remember the Metadata palette? Well the Keywords palette should be nested right behind it if you haven't changed your Panel area. If you have, then you can get back to where I am by choosing Window>Workspace>Reset to Default Workspace or pressing Command-F1 (PC: Control-F1). Then click on the Keywords tab in the bottom third of the Panel area to show that palette.

TURBO BOOST

When finding images using Bridge's search feature, keep the search results from opening in a new window by turning off the Show Find Results in a New Browser Window checkbox.

©MATT KLOSKOWSKI

©MATT KLOSKOWSKI

©MATT KLOSKOWSKI

STEP THREE:

Now it's time to add some keywords to the photos. If you look in the Keywords palette you'll see that Bridge has a set of default keywords in there for you. Already entered are a few common events, places, and people's names. In fact, my favorite feature is that Bridge automatically recognizes your and your family's names. It just so happens that my name is Matthew and my son's name is Ryan—I swear I'm not lying. Okay, maybe I am lying by saying that Bridge recognizes your family's names automatically. Something tells me I'm just lucky that Matthew and Ryan happened to be the default names in my version of Bridge. For example's sake, let's say you want to tag your photos with one of the default keywords. Just select the photos you want to keyword in Bridge (in my example, photos of my son Ryan), then click on the keyword in the Keywords palette, and it'll be assigned to those photos.

STEP FOUR:

Okay, now let's go out on a limb and assume that your family does not have anyone named Ryan or Matthew, or whichever default names appear in your version of Bridge (it's a crazy idea, isn't it?). Well, you can create a new keyword by just clicking on the small, right-facing triangle at the top right of the palette and choosing New Keyword from the flyout menu. Add a descriptive name for your keyword (such as Diana, for my wife) and then press Return (PC: Enter) to confirm it. After that, you can drag it into whatever category it best fits.

Learn the rating shortcuts, since they're really easy to remember. They all use the Command (PC: Control) key and the number of stars corresponds to the numbers 1–5.

STEP FIVE:

Now you can go on tagging your photos with keywords. By the way, you can also Control-click (PC: Right-click) on an existing keyword to rename it. However, I don't want to do that here because the existing keywords happen to work well for my family.

STEP SIX:

Okay, now that you've added keywords to your photos, it's time to see how to search for them. That's where the benefits of adding keywords really pay off. From the Bridge menu, choose Edit>Find. Even better, you can use the keyboard shortcut of Command-F (PC: Control-F). The Find dialog will appear.

STEP SEVEN:

First, you will need to choose a source in which to search for your images. The Look In menu will default to whatever folder you're currently in, but you can choose another folder from the pop-up menu, or click the Browse button. You can also choose to look in all subfolders that may be included inside of that folder by turning on the Include All Subfolders checkbox in the Source section.

TURBO BOOST

In Bridge, when you're browsing a folder of files you can click on any file in that folder, start typing the name of the file that you want to open, and Bridge will take you right to it.

STEP EIGHT:

Next, pick the criteria you want to use for this search from the first pop-up menu in the Criteria section. The default is File-name, which is good for finding photos by name, but in this case choose Keywords. In the second pop-up menu, leave the choice set to Contains. Then, in the last one enter "Ryan" or, on the off chance you don't have a son named Ryan like I do, type whatever keywords you've used.

STEP NINE:

Now, just click Find to start your search. By default, the Show Find Results in a New Browser Window checkbox is turned on, so your search results will open in a new Bridge window. In this case, all photos of my son Ryan that I tagged were displayed.

TURBO BOOST

If you accidentally remove any of the default folders from the Favorites palette, just go into Bridge's General Preferences and add them back in the Favorites Items section.

SAVING YOUR FAVORITE FOLDERS IN BRIDGE

I gotta say that the Favorites palette in Bridge is one of the smallest, but coolest little time-saving features. I often have a few folders that I use all of the time. Instead of always trying to find them, I just set them up as a favorite, and I always have quick access to them. Plus, there are already some useful shortcuts in there, such as one for Adobe Stock Photos, Bridge Center, and any saved collections.

STEP ONE:
Using Bridge, first make sure you can see the Favorites palette. If it's closed, then just choose View>Favorites Panel to add it to the top of the Panel area. Then, navigate to one of your most frequently used folders so you can see the folder in the central browser area.

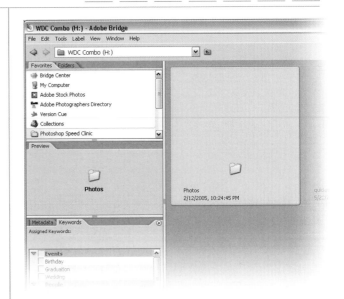

TURBO BOOST

To remove a favorite, Control-click (PC: Right-click) and choose **Remove From Favorites.**

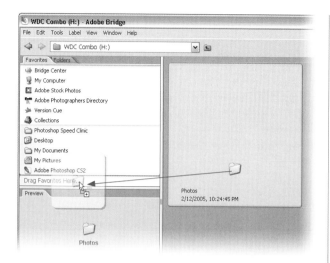

STEP TWO:

Once you find it, click on the folder and drag it to the Favorites palette. Be careful, though; you want to drag it in between or below any other favorite items in the palette. If you drag it inside another folder for instance, you'll just be relocating the folder, instead of creating a shortcut to it.

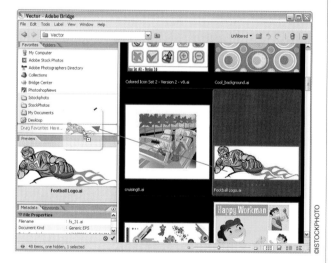

STEP THREE:

Don't stop there. If you find a favorite image or photo that you'd like to create a shortcut to, then just drag that over, as well. This works great if you have a logo file that you're using all of the time and always want quick access to it.

©ISTOCKPHOTO

Add your frequently used project files to Bridge's Favorites palette so you can easily get to them.

CHAPTER 2

ADDING AUTOMATION USING ACTIONS

THE BASICS OF STREAMLINING YOUR WORK WITH ACTIONS

Have you ever felt like there just aren't enough hours in the day to get all of your work done? Think of all the small, repetitive tasks that you do every day in Photoshop. Sure, some of them may require that you pick specific settings to make the image look right, but I'll bet that if you look at your Photoshop workflow you'll find many tasks that don't require your interaction. That's where actions come in. Actions are tiny little macros that record the changes and adjustments that you do in Photoshop. If you're reading this introduction and have heard of actions but are just not sure where to start, then this is it. Whether you just want to make your life easier or you want to start learning the secrets that the pros use to get things done faster, this chapter will give you the basics of what you'll need to start using actions in Photoshop.

RECORDING A SIMPLE ACTION TO AUTOMATE COMMON TASKS

I remember the first time I discovered actions in Photoshop. I was like a kid in a candy store. I was creating actions left and right and downloading them from every website possible (which wasn't many at the time). Needless to say, things have changed since then but I still love actions and I love to do cool things with them. But we have to start with the basics, so let's take a look at how to create a simple one-step action.

STEP ONE:

In Photoshop, open a photo that needs sharpening. We're going to create an action that not only sharpens this photo but will sharpen other photos for you, as well. If you don't already see the Actions palette, open it by choosing Window>Actions or press Option-F9 (PC: Alt-F9).

STEP TWO:

Now, click the Create New Action icon at the bottom of the palette to begin creating a new action. The New Action dialog will appear. Here's where you can enter a descriptive name for your action. For this example, call this action Sharpen Photos.

STEP THREE:

Choose which set you'd like to add this action to from the Set pop-up menu. A set is like a folder for actions—it helps keep them organized. You can just put this one into the Default Actions set for now.

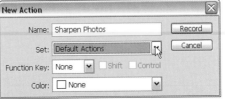

TURBO BOOST

If you use actions a lot, you'll probably begin to hate the shortcut for the Actions palette (Option-F9 [PC: Alt-F9]). Don't forget you can always change this under Edit>Keyboard Shortcuts.

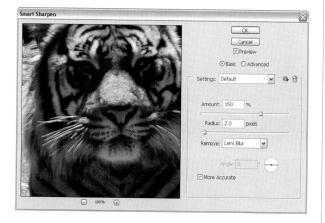

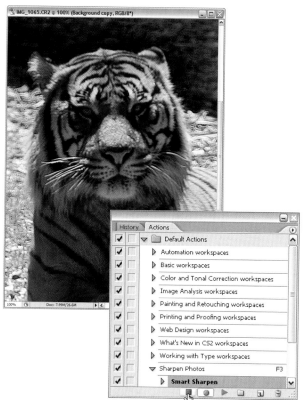

STEP FOUR:

Next, you can choose a function key to assign as a shortcut for your action. This will allow you to just press a single key to run your action, instead of always opening the Actions palette. Choose F3 from the Function Key pop-up menu for this action. Leave the Color setting to None, and click Record to start recording your action.

STEP FIVE:

You're now ready to start actually recording steps in the action. Since you already have a photo open from Step One, choose Filter>Sharpen>Smart Sharpen. In the Smart Sharpen dialog, in Basic mode, enter the following settings and click OK to close the dialog: Amount 150%, Radius 2, Remove Lens Blur, and turn on the More Accurate checkbox.

STEP SIX:

After you click OK, look in the Actions palette. You'll see that there is one step that has been recorded in the action for the Smart Sharpen filter. You can press the Stop Recording icon (it's the little square icon on the bottom left of the palette) to stop recording the action. Your photo is sharpened and the action is stored in the Actions palette. You can now open another photo and press F3 to run the action on it (remember, that was the shortcut key we assigned back in Step Four). Your photo will automatically get sharpened using the same settings and you won't have to lift a finger (well, you'll only have to lift one finger).

TURBO BOOST

Using the function keys as shortcuts for actions isn't always a possibility, especially when you're using a laptop. Try assigning the Command (PC: Control) and/or Shift key to give you a lot more options for shortcut keys.

CHANGING AN EXISTING ACTION

After I realized how cool actions were to create, I quickly found that once I created an action, I inevitably needed to make changes to it. For example, I noticed that while I was sharpening my photos I always made a duplicate layer of the photo to apply my sharpening changes to. That way I could always selectively erase parts of the layer (or better yet, use a layer mask) to remove any areas that may have been oversharpened. Luckily, editing an existing action is nearly as easy as creating a new one.

STEP ONE:
First, open a photo, then open the Actions palette, and find that action that you'd like to modify. For example, the Sharpen Photos action that was created in the previous tutorial has one step in it—a Smart Sharpen filter. We'll use that as a starting point here, so if you didn't do the previous tutorial, go do it now (it only takes a minute or two).

METHOD ONE: MODIFYING AN ACTION SETTING

STEP ONE:
Double-click on the Smart Sharpen step in the Actions palette. Nothing will really change at this point, but once the dialog opens, recording will begin on the changes to this action.

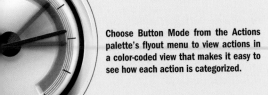

TURBO BOOST

Choose Button Mode from the Actions palette's flyout menu to view actions in a color-coded view that makes it easy to see how each action is categorized.

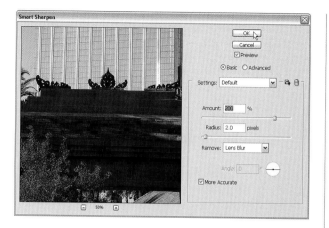

STEP TWO:

In the Smart Sharpen dialog, change the Amount setting from 150% to 200%, and click OK. You've just modified the action's settings and every time you run this action the Smart Sharpen filter will use 200% instead of 150%. Just expand the step to see the modification in the Actions palette.

METHOD TWO: ADDING A STEP TO AN ACTION

STEP ONE:

Click once on the Smart Sharpen step in the Actions palette to select it. Press the Record icon at the bottom of the Actions palette to start recording again. Now duplicate the layer with the photo on it by pressing Command-J (PC: Control-J). If you look in the Actions palette, you'll see that another step has been added to the action.

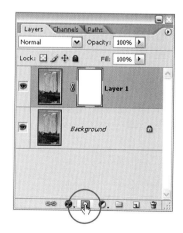

STEP TWO:

You could stop here, but go ahead and add a layer mask to this layer by clicking on the Add Layer Mask icon at the bottom of the Layers palette.

When creating an action you can assign a color to it so you (or anyone you share it with) can easily find the action when in Button mode.

THE PHOTOSHOP CS2 SPEED CLINIC   CHAPTER 2

STEP THREE:

Press the Stop Recording icon. You're done recording the additions to the action, but one thing you'll notice is that the steps are not in the correct order. To fix this just drag the Smart Sharpen step to the bottom of the Sharpen Photos action's steps.

Before

After

STEP FOUR:

Now you can run the action on another photo and it will automatically create a duplicate layer of the photo with a layer mask, before it runs the Smart Sharpen filter. Then you can always use the layer mask to erase away oversharpened areas, or reduce the opacity of the sharpened duplicate if you find the photo was sharpened too much.

TURBO BOOST

When troubleshooting actions, choose Playback Options from the Actions palette's flyout menu and select Pause For. Enter 3 seconds. The action will run slowly, but you can watch it more easily and figure out where problems are.

It wasn't long after I started creating actions that I realized I wanted to be able to do a couple of things. First, I had a computer at home and a computer at work and I wanted to be able to use my actions on both of them, without re-creating them from scratch. Next, I had friends and co-workers that wanted to use the same actions, so I quickly found the advantages of being able to save and load actions.

SAVING AND SHARING YOUR ACTIONS

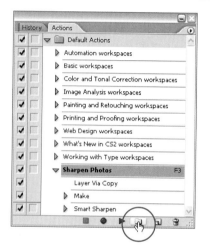

STEP ONE:
For this example, let's save the Sharpen Photos action that we created back in the previous two tutorials. Here's the problem when saving actions, though. Actions need to be saved in a set. You can't save actions individually. Well, you can but they still must be in a set—even if it's only one action. To create a set for our Sharpen Photos action, click the Create New Set icon (it looks like a little folder) at the bottom of the Actions palette. In the New Set dialog, name the set Sharpen Photos, and click OK. You'll see a new folder (set) appear in the Actions palette.

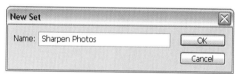

STEP TWO:
Drag the Sharpen Photos action into the set by clicking on it and dragging it on top of the newly created set (with the folder icon). This enables us to save the action.

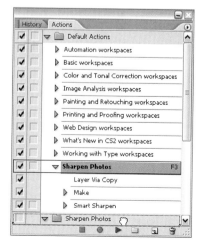

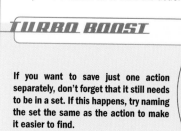

TURBO BOOST

If you want to save just one action separately, don't forget that it still needs to be in a set. If this happens, try naming the set the same as the action to make it easier to find.

STEP THREE:

Click once on the Sharpen Photos set. Then click the small, right-facing triangle at the top right of the Actions palette. From the palette's flyout menu, choose Save Actions, and the Save dialog will appear.

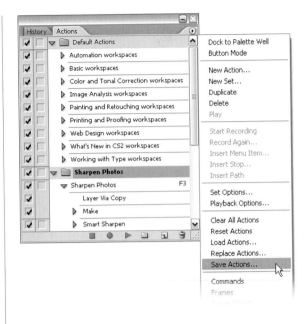

STEP FOUR:

In the Save dialog, choose a location for the action. It's usually best to place them into the Photoshop Actions folder (in Adobe Photoshop CS2's Presets folder) with the other actions, but you can choose somewhere else if you'd like. Then click the Save button, and the action will be saved.

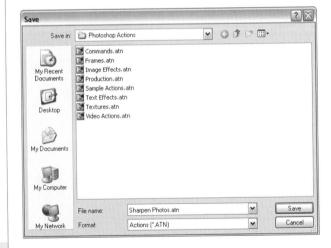

TURBO BOOST

Save your actions in Photoshop CS2's Photoshop Actions folder, in the Presets folder, and they'll appear in your Actions palette's flyout menu so you can quickly load them the next time you restart Photoshop.

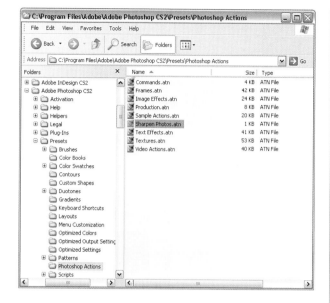

STEP FIVE:

To share this action with other people, just copy and provide the Sharpen Photos.atn file to whomever you're sharing the action with. They'll be able to load it right into Photoshop and use it the same way you did (see the next tutorial to find out how).

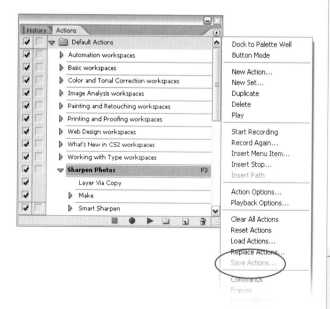

You can't save an action unless it's located inside of a set, and you have to click on that set before you try to save the action. If you click on an action, Save Actions will be grayed out on the Actions palette's flyout menu. Yep, even if you just want to save one action you first need to create a new set or put it into an existing set. Sorry, I didn't make the rules here.

You can quickly load an action into Photoshop by navigating to the action in Adobe Bridge and double-clicking it.

LOADING ACTIONS FROM OTHER PEOPLE

This is a continuation of the previous tutorial on saving and sharing actions. After all, what good is saving a new action without knowing how to load it? Also, if you're working with actions a lot, it's likely you'll be downloading them from websites such as the Adobe Studio Exchange (http://share.studio.adobe.com). You'll need to know how to get those actions into Photoshop so that you can use them.

STEP ONE:
Before you load an action, make sure you have an action to load. This could be an action that someone else has given you, one that you've saved and are relocating to another computer, or one that you've downloaded from the Web. Whatever the source, the action will be a file with a name and an ATN extension. Make sure that you have that action somewhere on your computer.

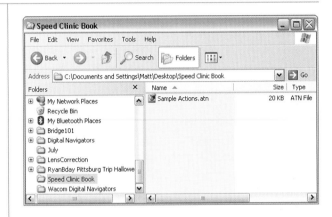

STEP TWO:
To load the action in Photoshop, click the small, right-facing triangle at the top right of the Actions palette. From the flyout menu, choose Load Actions and you'll see the Load dialog appear.

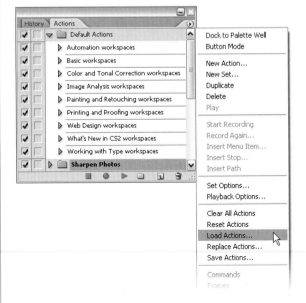

TURBO BOOST

If you want to quickly get your Actions palette back to the way it was when you loaded Photoshop, just choose Reset Actions from the Actions palette's flyout menu.

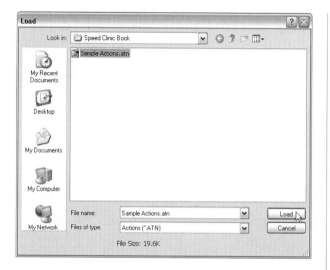

STEP THREE:
Locate the action file that you've previously saved or that someone else has given you. It should have an ATN file extension after the name. (Honestly, the only files that should even appear in this dialog have that extension after it, so you shouldn't have to worry.) Once you locate the action in the Load dialog, select it, and click Load to load it into the Actions palette.

STEP FOUR:
You should now see the action set in the Actions palette and if you expand the set, you'll see the action (or actions) that belong to that set. Now, you're free to use it just as you would any other action.

TURBO BOOST

Get rid of that annoying red eye with a new tool in Photoshop CS2 called the Red Eye tool. It's nested under the Spot Healing Brush tool, and all you need to do is click once on the red eye to remove it.

CHAPTER 3

CREATING SMARTER ACTIONS

MAKE ACTIONS THAT NOT ONLY WORK QUICKLY BUT ARE SMARTER, TOO

Creating actions is one thing. They're great timesavers, and they keep us from having to do a lot of repetitive and mundane tasks. But...creating smart actions is an entirely different ballgame. While actions on their own can do so much for your productivity, there's a lot more to them than what you see on the surface. The good news is that once you learn these techniques, the sky is the limit. You'll have what you need to start not only creating actions that make you work faster, but creating actions that help make decisions for you and let you get on with the important stuff.

CREATING ACTIONS WITH A ONE-CLICK UNDO

Okay, I know this one sounds weird, but trust me, this is one heck of a trick when you're working with actions. Imagine this... suppose you create an action that has over 50 steps. Now, let's say you open a photo and do a few fixes to it before you run the action—maybe some retouching, resizing, or cropping. Next, you run the action but realize you want to undo it. What?! There's no undo button for an action! And your History palette is full because there were too many steps in the action. That's where creating a one-click undo helps out. Here's how.

STEP ONE:
Open any image in Photoshop. Then choose Window>Actions to open the Actions palette (or just press Option-F9 [PC: Alt-F9]) and click the Create New Action icon at the bottom of the palette. From the New Action dialog, enter a meaningful name for this action, and click Record to start recording.

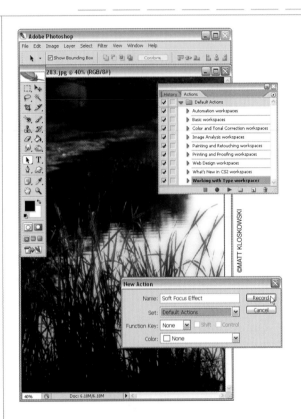

©MATT KLOSKOWSKI

STEP TWO:
Go to the History palette (Window> History) and from the palette's flyout menu, choose New Snapshot. In the New Snapshot dialog, just leave the default name and click OK.

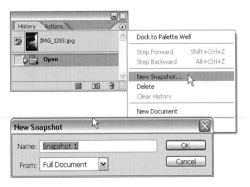

Step Three:

Now, go back to the Actions palette. Notice the first step that has been inserted at the top of your action? It's a brand new History State snapshot of your image that will be taken before the Action is played. You can now go on recording your action just as you normally would (here, I created an action that adds a soft focus effect to an image). Press the Stop Recording button when you're done.

Before

Step Four:

Go ahead and run your action on an image by clicking the Play Selection icon. After it's finished, take a look in the History palette and you'll see a new snapshot. Just click that snapshot in the History palette to go back to the way your image was before you ran the action. No matter how many steps were in the action, you'll always be able to undo it with one click.

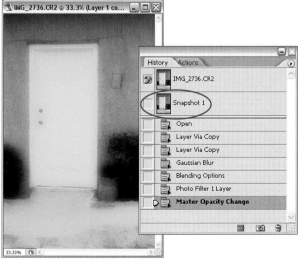

After

Press-and-hold Command-Option (PC: Control-Alt) when you choose Save Actions to save your actions in a text file. You can then use this file to review or print the contents of an action.

RECORDING MENU ITEMS IN AN ACTION

Even though we can do a ton of things with actions, there is always one thing that stumps people—inserting or recording certain menu items. For example, if you try to record the View>Show>All command (this shows all extras that may be included in a Photoshop file, such as guides, rulers, smart guides, etc.), Photoshop will not play that step back when you run the action. There's an easy fix, though; you just need to know where to look.

STEP ONE:
We're going to record an action that sets up an open image to make it easier to work with. This action will fit the image onscreen, turn snapping on, and show all information and extras that may be inside of a Photoshop file—all of which are functions under the View menu that just can't be recorded by using the menu in an action. Now, you could always press Command-Shift-; (PC: Control-Shift-;) to turn snapping on, choose View>Show>All, and then press Command-0 (PC: Control-0) to fit onscreen, but that's a pain in the neck. An action is much better. So, let's get started by opening any image. Create a new action, name it "Document Setup," and click Record in the New Action dialog to start recording.

STEP TWO:
Go ahead and choose View>Show>All. Take note of the Actions palette as you do this. You will notice that no step is inserted into the action when you make this choice. That is because Photoshop didn't record it.

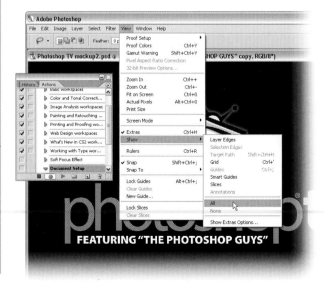

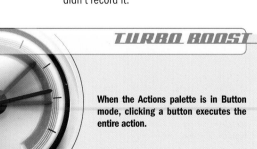

TURBO BOOST

When the Actions palette is in Button mode, clicking a button executes the entire action.

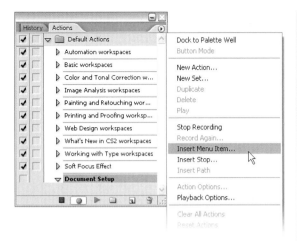

Step Three:

To make this work, from the Actions palette's flyout menu choose Insert Menu Item. You'll see the Insert Menu Item dialog appear showing that no menu item has been selected yet.

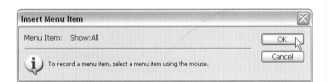

Step Four:

Now this sounds odd, but to use this dialog you actually don't do anything with it. Instead, go to the menu bar and choose View>Show>All again. The dialog will then update with the Menu Item you've picked. Click OK to close the dialog.

Step Five:

If you now look in your Actions palette, you'll see that the Document Setup action has been updated with a new step.

If you haven't figured it out yet, you can't use the Move tool in an action—it simply won't be recorded. To get around this, go into Free Transform mode first by pressing Command-T (PC: Control-T) and then move your object.

STEP SIX:

Follow Steps Three and Four to add the menu commands for View>Snap and View>Fit on Screen to your action. Click the Stop Recording icon to finish your action. From the Actions palette's flyout menu, choose Actions Options and set the action up with a shortcut key (which can also be done when you first create the action). Now, every time you want to see all of the extras inside of your Photoshop images, you can just press that shortcut key.

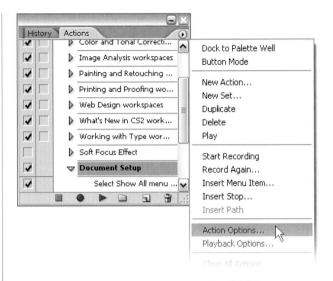

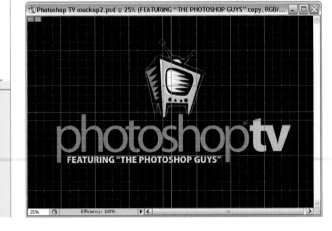

The first time I shared an action with my co-workers it was a doozy. It was a great action but it had plenty of steps in it and required the interaction of the user at certain times. All day long, people came up to me telling me the action had stopped or they didn't know what to do to finish it. That's when I realized the importance of adding pop-up messages to the action to help people along. It's also a great way to plug yourself or your website if you share your actions on the Web.

ADDING MESSAGES AND NOTIFICATIONS TO AN ACTION

©MATT KLOSKOWSKI

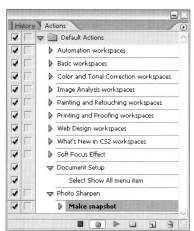

STEP ONE:
Open an image and create a new action by clicking the Create New Action icon at the bottom of the Actions palette. Call it "Photo Sharpen" and click the Record button to start recording.

STEP TWO:
Earlier in this chapter, there was a tutorial on creating a one-click undo for all of your actions. For the first step in this action, go to the History palette and from the palette's flyout menu, choose New Snapshot. This will make it so your new action will have a one-click undo.

TURBO BOOST

You can play a single command in an action by pressing-and-holding the Command (PC: Control) key and double-clicking on the command in the action.

STEP THREE:

Now, the problem is that people who use this action may not know about this step, so let's tell them about it. Go back to the Actions palette and from the palette's flyout menu, choose Insert Stop.

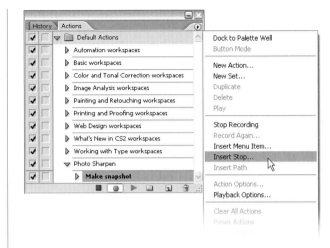

STEP FOUR:

You'll see a Record Stop dialog open. Here you can type messages to the user. Go ahead and enter a message letting them know that if they finish running the action and want to undo it, they can always go to the History palette and click on the second snapshot in the palette to get back to where they were before they ran the action. You also want them to be able to continue to run this action, so turn on the Allow Continue checkbox. If you don't check this option, then the action will stop and the user will have to press the Play Selection icon to continue running the action. Press OK when you're done.

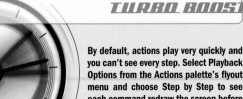
TURBO BOOST

By default, actions play very quickly and you can't see every step. Select Playback Options from the Actions palette's flyout menu and choose Step by Step to see each command redraw the screen before going to the next command.

STEP FIVE:
Continue recording your action just as you normally would. Here, I'm just going to sharpen the photo using the Smart Sharpen filter, but this could just as easily be many more steps.

STEP SIX:
Right before you're about to click the Stop Recording icon, it's a good idea to add another message to the user letting them know who you are and maybe even adding some copyright information. From the Actions palette's flyout menu, choose Insert Stop, just like you did in Step Three. Enter a message telling the user where to find out more information about you and any copyright info, as well. This time, though, don't click Allow Continue. This is the last step, so it's okay to just stop the action right here. Click OK to close the dialog, click the Stop Recording icon in the Actions palette, and you're done.

TURBO BOOST

In the new Smart Sharpen filter, if you find you have specific settings in Smart Sharpen that you really like then go ahead and save them. To save settings, click on the small disk icon next to the Settings pop-up menu.

STEP SEVEN:

Now any time the action is run, a dialog will pop up with your message letting users know that you added a one-click undo to the action. Simply press Continue to continue running the action.

STEP EIGHT:

Right before the action finishes, another dialog will pop up with all of your info. Click Stop and you're done. You've just created an action that is a lot faster, easier, and more user friendly.

Message

This action was created by Matt Kloskowski. Copyright 2005 Matt Kloskowski.
Thanks for using this action and please visit my website at www.photoshopuser.com :)

Stop

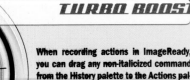

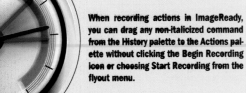

TURBO BOOST

When recording actions in ImageReady, you can drag any non-italicized command from the History palette to the Actions palette without clicking the Begin Recording icon or choosing Start Recording from the flyout menu.

This is one of the most important tutorials in this book. I know this is a bold statement but after you learn how to do this, you'll unlock a ton of mystery that surrounds actions. The first time I recorded an action to add a watermark to my photos, I was extremely disappointed with the results. You see, some of the photos were portrait oriented and some were landscape. Basically, I had a lot of different image sizes and dimensions, but I wanted one action to add a watermark to all of them.

CREATING A WATERMARK ACTION FOR ANY IMAGE ORIENTATION

Incorrect

©MATT KLOSKOWSKI

Correct

THE PROBLEM WITH SPECIFIC IMAGE COORDINATES IN ACTIONS:

When you record an action that places, say, a watermark in the center of an image, the action actually records the exact coordinates in which you place that watermark. This is fine if you always play the action on images that are all the same exact size and orientation as the one in which you recorded the action. Since this isn't always the case, this issue presents our action with a problem in a big way, especially if the symbol is created in an area of the image that doesn't exist in other images. Here's the trick: You first need to place your watermark in the image in a way that Photoshop will recognize it no matter what type of image you're working with. Next, you need to use Photoshop's automatic alignment features to center the watermark so that no matter what the final dimensions of your image are, it'll still be in the center. Let's take a look at how we can do this.

TURBO BOOST

If an action won't load in Photoshop or ImageReady, make sure that it was intended for that specific program. Photoshop actions are not compatible with ImageReady, and vice versa.

STEP ONE:

Open a photo to which you'd like to add a watermark. First, let's insert the watermark shape. Don't worry, though, we don't have to start recording yet. In this example, I'm using a custom shape that comes with Photoshop CS2. It's the copyright symbol. Select the Custom Shape tool (press Shift-U until you get it), then in the Options Bar, click the Shape thumbnail, and from the resulting Custom Shape Picker, click the copyright symbol.

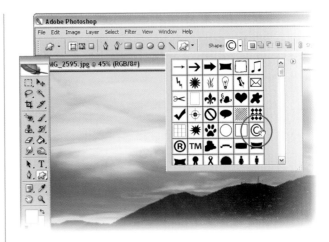

STEP TWO:

Next, in the Options Bar, click Paths (it's the third icon from the left and looks like a square with the Pen tool icon in it). This tells Photoshop that you want to create the custom shape using a path only and not a shape layer or pixels.

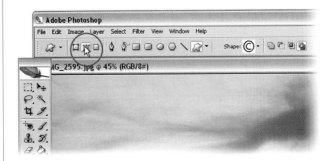

STEP THREE:

Now, press-and-hold the Shift key (this makes sure the proportions stay correct) and draw a copyright symbol anywhere on the image.

Don't worry that we haven't started recording an action at this point. If we recorded the drawing of the copyright custom shape, then every time someone ran this action, they would need to have

the same copyright symbol shape set loaded. If they didn't, Photoshop would give them a nasty error dialog and the action wouldn't work. We're going to get around that in Step Eight by inserting a path into the action.

STEP FOUR:

As I mentioned in the opening, depending on the size and orientation of your image, the exact coordinates of where you placed this copyright symbol may or may not exist in the image that you run this action on. To get around this we're going to use a little trick. First, press Command-T (PC: Control-T) to go into Free Transform mode. Then in the Options Bar, on the Reference Point Location icon, click on the top left white square. Finally, set the X and Y coordinates to 0. This will place the logo in the top-left corner of the image.

STEP FIVE:

Okay, now you're ready to actually start recording the action. In the Actions palette, click the Create New Action icon at the bottom right of the palette. Name the action "Add Watermark" and click Record to start recording the action.

TURBO BOOST

When an image is open in Photoshop, click the small, right-facing triangle in the status bar at the bottom of the document window, and choose Reveal in Bridge to quickly find the folder in which it's saved.

STEP SIX:

In Step Three, you created the copyright symbol. Let's insert this symbol into the action now as a path, so you never actually have to have that custom shape loaded on the computer. Go over to the Paths palette. Unless you've changed your palette layout, it should be nested beneath the Layers palette.

STEP SEVEN:

From the Toolbox, select the Path Selection tool (A). Then click once on the copyright symbol to select the path. Now, you should see all of the anchor points that make up the path.

STEP EIGHT:

From the Actions palette's flyout menu, choose Insert Path. This actually records the entire path itself into the action. No custom shapes are added, so anyone can use this action.

TURBO BOOST

If you look at Photoshop's Sample Actions set, you'll see that some include a parenthesis after the name (i.e., selection, layer, type). These are hints that something, such as a selection, is required to run the action.

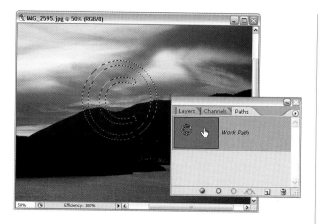

STEP NINE:

Now, we need to turn this path into pixels. In the Paths palette, Command-click (PC: Control-click) on the Work Path thumbnail. This will turn the path into a selection.

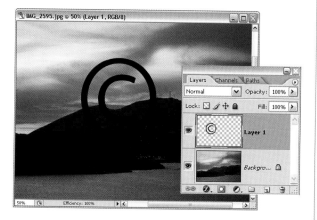

STEP TEN:

Go back over to the Layers palette. Create a new layer by clicking on the Create a New Layer icon at the bottom right of the palette. Press D to set your Foreground color to black. Finally, press Option-Delete (PC: Alt-Backspace) to fill the selection with black. Press Command-D (PC: Control-D) to Deselect.

STEP ELEVEN:

Next, to place the logo in the exact center of the document press Command-A (PC: Control-A) to Select All. Choose Layer>Align Layers To Selection>Vertical Centers. Then choose Layer>Align Layers To Selection>Horizontal Centers. This will put the watermark in the exact center of the image no matter what the image dimensions are. Press Command-D (PC: Control-D) to Deselect.

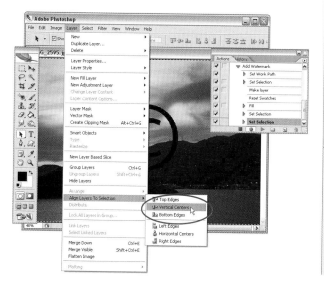

TURBO BOOST

Do yourself a favor and make sure you save any custom actions you've created by choosing Save Action from the Actions palette's flyout menu. If you don't and Photoshop quits unexpectedly, you may lose your actions and all the work you've done.

STEP TWELVE:

Now, it's time to add the watermark style. Double-click on the copyright layer to bring up the Layer Style dialog, click on Bevel and Emboss along the left side of the dialog to turn on the checkbox. You can leave the default settings, or if you're the type that always needs to tweak things (hey, you know who you are), then feel free to adjust the settings here. Don't click OK yet.

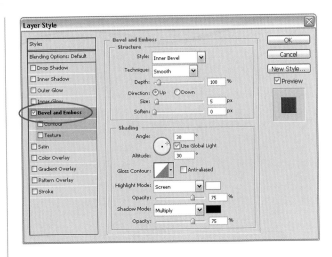

STEP THIRTEEN:

Next, click on Blending Options (at the top left of the dialog), and in the Advanced Blending section, drop the Fill Opacity setting down to 0%. This should remove all of the color from the watermark but leave the beveled see-through appearance intact. Now, click OK.

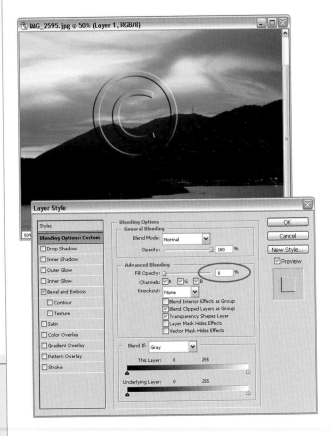

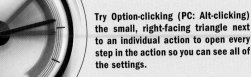

TURBO BOOST

Try Option-clicking (PC: Alt-clicking) the small, right-facing triangle next to an individual action to open every step in the action so you can see all of the settings.

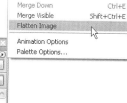

©MATT KLOSKOWSKI

STEP FOURTEEN:

To wrap things up, go to the Paths palette and drag the Work Path to the Trash icon to delete it. We don't need it anymore and there's no reason to save it. Then in the Layers palette, choose Flatten Image from the palette's flyout menu, to flatten all layers.

Make sure you delete the Work Path before you flatten the image and stop recording. If you don't, when you run the action on a new photo, you will end up with both the original copyright path and the centered watermark.

TURBO BOOST

You can also Option-click (PC: Alt-click) on the action set to unfurl every action and each step within each action.

STEP FIFTEEN:

Press Stop Recording and you're done. Whew! That was a long one but worth it. Now you can open any image (any size or orientation) and run this action on it. You can give the action to someone else who doesn't even have that copyright custom shape loaded and they can run it, too. Better yet, use your own watermark in Step Three (which other computers are not likely to have) and you'll really start to see the power of inserting a path into an action.

TURBO BOOST

Bet you didn't know that you can create an action that plays another action. As you're recording an action, just go to the Actions palette, select the action you want to include, and press the Play Selection icon.

I think the way Photoshop names this feature doesn't really do it justice. Photoshop calls this a "conditional" action, which sounds too much like a techie term. Why not call it what it does? It makes a decision for you. This only works in ImageReady, so if you're someone other than a Web designer, there's a chance you may never have even opened ImageReady. The cool thing is that you don't need to be a Web designer to take advantage of ImageReady's features. You can do a lot of the same things using its Actions features.

CREATING AN ACTION THAT MAKES DECISIONS FOR YOU

WHY USE A CONDITIONAL ACTION?

Let's say someone hands you a CD with hundreds of photos of all types and sizes that need to be put onto a Web gallery or catalog site. Some are already small and can be put onto the site, while some are too large and must be resized. So, you decide to write an action that sizes (using Image Size) the large photos down to 640x480 at the most. However, if you run the action on all of the photos on the CD and some of those photos are smaller than 640x480, those images will be enlarged since the Image Size change will run on every file, and you don't want that. So, what's left? Do you go through the images and pick out all the ones that are already small? Nope, just open ImageReady and create a conditional action.

STEP ONE:

First off, we need to open ImageReady. If you've already got Photoshop open, it's easy: just click the Edit in ImageReady icon at the bottom of the Toolbox or press Command-Shift-M (PC: Control-Shift-M). ImageReady will launch and as soon as it does, open any photo to use for recording an action.

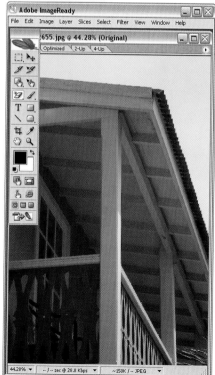

TURBO BOOST

Actions tend to rely on previous steps. Therefore, deselecting or removing a step will likely break the action.

STEP TWO:

To display the Actions palette in Image-Ready just choose Window>Actions. The palette works very similar to the way the Actions palette does in Photoshop, so just click the Create New Action icon at the bottom right of the palette to start recording an action. Name the Action "Web Gallery Resize," leave the Function Key field at None, and click Record.

STEP THREE:

To resize this image choose Image>Image Size. In the Image Size dialog, enter 640 pixels for the Width setting—or whatever maximum width that you want for your images. Also, turn on the Action Options checkbox at the bottom of the dialog and choose Width for the Fit Image By setting. Click OK.

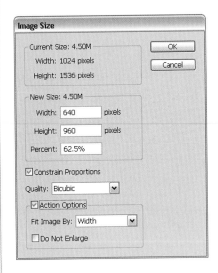

STEP FOUR:

Now, we need to make sure the height of the image doesn't exceed 480 pixels, so choose Image>Image Size again. This time set the Height to 480 pixels. Again, turn on the Action Options checkbox, and this time select Height for the Fit Image By setting. Click OK.

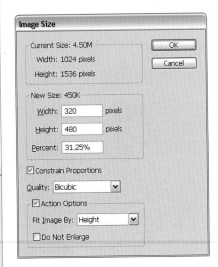

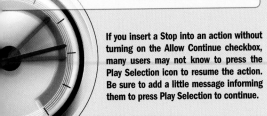

TURBO BOOST

If you insert a Stop into an action without turning on the Allow Continue checkbox, many users may not know to press the Play Selection icon to resume the action. Be sure to add a little message informing them to press Play Selection to continue.

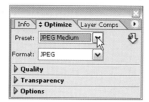

STEP FIVE:

Next, let's save this image for the Web. Since these are all going to be photos, let's save them as JPEG files. Go to the Optimize palette—it should be nested with the Info palette. If you don't see the palette, go to Window>Optimize to open it. From the Preset pop-up menu, select JPEG Medium so the file sizes aren't too big.

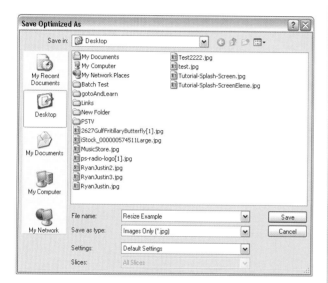

STEP SIX:

Then choose File>Save Optimized As. Keep in mind that this is just a dummy file and it doesn't really matter where we save this image. If it's one of your original files you may want to make sure that you don't overwrite the original.

STEP SEVEN:

Now, you're done recording so just click the Stop Recording icon at the bottom of the Actions palette.

TURBO BOOST

Here's a tip worth its weight in gold. When you're targeting various layers in an action, make sure you use the commands under Layer > Arrange to move layers. If you don't, your action may fail when used on another file.

STEP EIGHT:

It's time to insert the conditional steps into the action to help make decisions for us. At the bottom of the Actions palette, click the Insert a Step icon (it's the one on the left) and choose Insert Conditional from the pop-up menu.

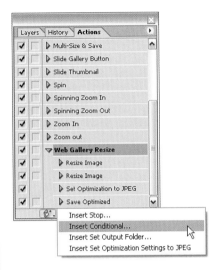

STEP NINE:

In the Conditional dialog, in the If the Following Condition Is Met section, choose Image Width from the first pop-up menu. Choose Is Greater Than from the second pop-up menu and enter 640 in the field to the right. (Remember, that is the maximum width that we want for our images.) In the Perform the Following Action section, choose Include from the pop-up menu and enter 1 step. Click OK.

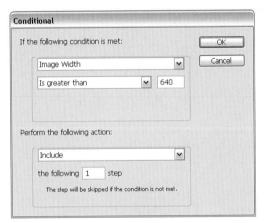

STEP TEN:

This will add another step to the end of your action. To make it work correctly, we want it above the first Resize Image step, so just click-and-drag it there now.

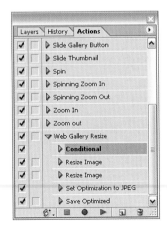

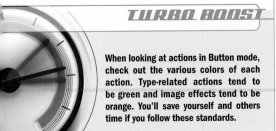

TURBO BOOST

When looking at actions in Button mode, check out the various colors of each action. Type-related actions tend to be green and image effects tend to be orange. You'll save yourself and others time if you follow these standards.

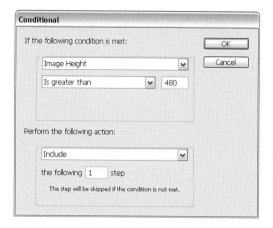

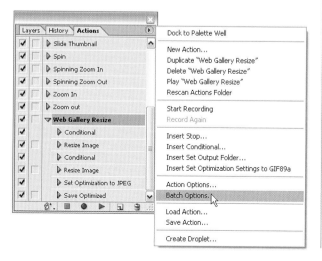

STEP ELEVEN:

Now, repeat Step Nine but this time, from the first pop-up menu in the If the Following Condition Is Met section, choose Image Height. Also, enter 480 (the maximum height that we want for our images) in the field to the right of the second pop-up menu. Leave all other fields with the settings we chose earlier and click OK. Once again, this will add the step to the wrong part of the action, so just click-and-drag it above the second Resize Image step but below the first one.

STEP TWELVE:

That's it. The Conditional action is now re-corded and it'll make the decisions for you. You can try it out on individual images but, honestly, the real power comes from using it in a droplet or batch process. Check out the tutorial on page 143 to see how to turn this into a droplet (a little program that will allow you to apply this action to an entire folder of images) and check out Chapter 4 to learn all about batch processing.

 You can't use ImageReady actions in Photoshop, so you'll need to run any batch processing tasks here in ImageReady. However, Photoshop's Batch feature is equally as powerful and Chapter 4 is devoted to it entirely.

TURBO BOOST

One thing you'll need to keep reminding yourself is that Adobe Bridge is not the Photoshop File Browser. In fact, you can open multiple Bridge windows by choosing File>New Window or by pressing Command-N (PC: Control-N).

CHAPTER **4**

APPLYING ACTIONS TO MULTIPLE IMAGES

UNCOVER THE SECRETS BEHIND PHOTOSHOP'S BATCH FEATURE

Batch processing is one of the most powerful things that you can do to speed up your work in Photoshop. It's so important that I've devoted an entire chapter to it instead of just making this a tutorial in another chapter (crazy I know, but hey, it's my book). So why would I do such a thing? Well, other than the obvious answer (which, by the way, is still "It's my book"), I made this its own chapter because I rarely have only one image that needs an action applied to it. More often, I've got hundreds of them. For example, if you're a photographer and you've got a whole photo shoot that you want to apply the same action to, or if you're a designer and you want to get a bunch of images ready for print, batch processing is the way to go and I want to make sure it gets plenty of attention here.

EVERYTHING YOU WANTED TO KNOW ABOUT BATCH PROCESSING

As I mentioned in the chapter introduction, this chapter is going to consist of nothing but batch processing. Yep, one giant, humongous, tell-ya-everything-about-it chapter. I did this because I wanted to cover everything about batch processing—every setting, dialog, and even some troubleshooting tips—because it's one of the most misunderstood (but most powerful) tools in Photoshop.

HOW TO USE THIS CHAPTER:
Before we start, I'll give you a quick rundown on how this chapter is going to go. I've broken the first tutorial up into sections based on the Batch dialog. We're going to go over everything—yes, I mean *everything*. That way, we make sure you know how to use each feature.

After that, there's a tutorial that puts all of this information to use and walks you through a batch-processing sample. So, if you're the type that likes to put things together without reading the instruction manual, or will never stop and ask for directions when you're lost (come on, you know you're out there), then you can just jump to page 71 and start that tutorial. You can always refer back to the explanation part if you want more info on a specific setting. If you'd rather get a bird's eye view of the entire Batch dialog first, then start here. Sound good? Let's get to it.

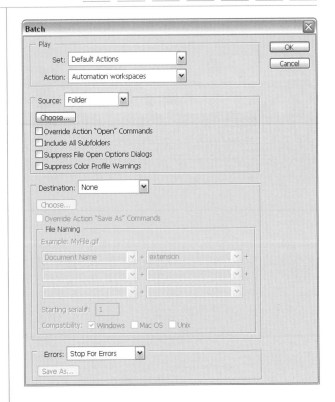

TURBO BOOST

You can improve batch performance by reducing the number of saved History States in Photoshop's Preferences, and by turning off the Automatically Create First Snapshot checkbox in the History palette's options on the flyout menu.

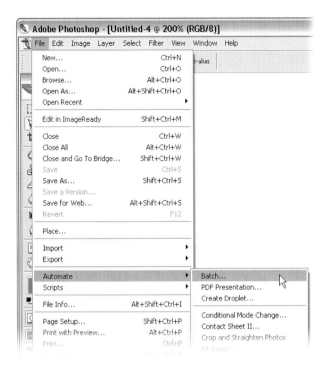

STARTING A BATCH PROCESS

OPTION ONE:

This one is my least favorite but I have to tell you about it anyway. In Photoshop, choose File>Automate>Batch. This will open the Batch dialog. When you use this method, you can choose a source folder of images to batch or you can choose to batch process any opened images. However, you can't select specific images from a folder or multiple folders (unless they're subfolders of the original folder).

TURBO BOOST

In Photoshop, choose History Options from the History palette's flyout menu and make sure the Make Layer Visibility Changes Undoable checkbox is turned on. This will save a History State even when you show or hide a layer.

OPTION TWO:

I recommend that you open Adobe Bridge and select the images you want to batch. You can even do a search that returns images from folders all over your hard drive, then batch all of them in one shot by choosing Tools>Photoshop>Batch. You just can't do that in Photoshop, which is why I recommend using Batch from Bridge. This will open the same dialog, except for the fact that the Source field will already have Bridge selected. You can also choose any of the other Source options that you can select when running Batch in Photoshop.

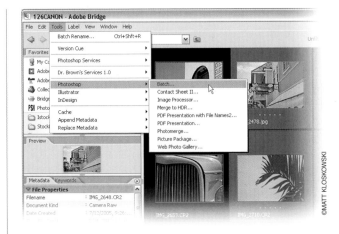

©MATT KLOSKOWSKI

PLAY (CHOOSING WHICH ACTION TO RUN):

Once the Batch dialog is open, the first thing you'll need to do is pick which action you want to run in this batch.

Set and Action: In the first section of the dialog, Play, choose which action you want to run from the pop-up menus. Choose the set that contains the action, and then choose the actual action itself from the Action pop-up menu.

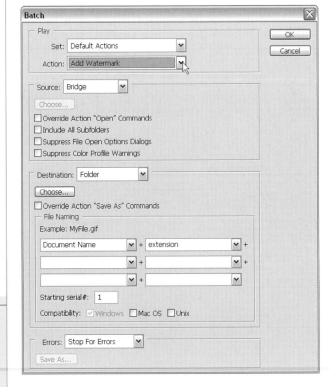

TURBO BOOST

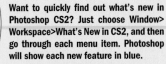

Want to quickly find out what's new in Photoshop CS2? Just choose Window> Workspace>What's New in CS2, and then go through each menu item. Photoshop will show each new feature in blue.

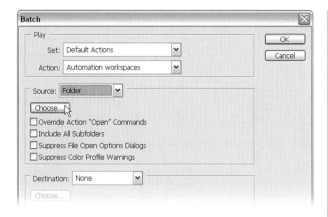

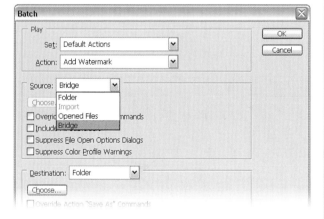

SOURCE (CHOOSING WHICH FILES TO BATCH):

Depending on which option you used to open the Batch dialog, you may only have certain options here.

Folder: If you opened the Batch dialog from either Photoshop or Bridge, then you can choose a folder here. If you select Folder from the pop-up menu, then the Choose button below will become enabled and you can pick which folder you want to batch.

Import: Choose Import to process images from a digital camera, scanner, or a PDF document.

Opened Files: Use this option if you have all of the files you want to batch already open in Photoshop. Honestly, this probably won't happen too often and you may find you never use this option.

Bridge: If you chose the Bridge method to launch the Batch dialog, then this field should already be populated with Bridge, and any selected photos will be batch processed.

TURBO BOOST

The Import option in the Source list will only work in Windows if you've got a digital camera or your scanner possesses a plug-in module that supports actions. In Mac OS, ImageReady also supports PICT format files.

Override Action "Open" Commands:
This is where a lot of people get confused. Many times, an action will contain an Open command. If it does, and you batch process multiple images using that action, it will open the same file every single time. Since that's probably not what you want, be sure to check this option and Photoshop will open only the images specified under Source.

Include All Subfolders: Check this option if you've got more folders within the main Source folder you picked.

Suppress File Open Options Dialogs: This option keeps any Open dialogs from popping up throughout the process (I highly recommend you check this option). For example, let's say you've got a bunch of Camera Raw files and you decide to batch process them to add a watermark and size them down for the Web. If you don't want the batch process to show the Camera Raw dialog for each photo and make you click Open, then you'll definitely want to choose this option.

Suppress Color Profile Warnings: This is a lot like the previous option. This one bypasses any color policy dialogs that may appear when opening an image. We've all seen this dialog and checking this option is the way to avoid it if you're batch processing.

TURBO BOOST

If you have created a batch process to run on hundreds of files, you'd better try it out on just a few first. It's an easy way to troubleshoot any problems that can arise and you'll save yourself a lot of time if something goes wrong.

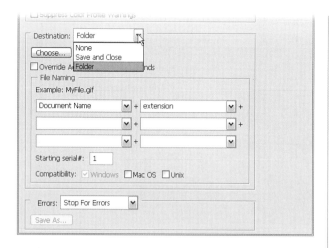

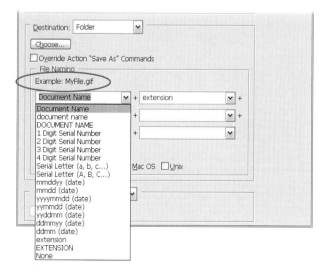

DESTINATION (CHOOSING HOW AND WHERE TO SAVE YOUR FILES):

Here you'll choose how and where you want to save your newly processed images.

None: Choose None if your action opens and saves the files you need it to and you don't need to save them anywhere. Chances are it won't, so you'll probably barely ever use this option.

Save and Close: This resaves the file in the same format and with the same settings as when it was opened, and closes it.

Folder: Choose Folder if you'd like to save the images from the batch into a specific location, other than where they were opened from. If you select this option, the Choose button will become enabled, allowing you to pick a folder.

Override Action "Save As" Commands:
Checking this option will ignore the Save As commands in the action. For instance, let's say you saved your image for the Web with specific JPEG settings. You want your batch processed files to be saved with those settings; however, you don't want every single file to be saved using exactly the same name, so you'd go ahead and check this setting.

FILE NAMING:

If you choose Folder as your destination, this section will become enabled. There's a lot of flexibility when it comes to naming the files here. Keep in mind that you can preview the proposed file name directly in the dialog, as well.

TURBO BOOST

If you're using a Function key as a shortcut for an action, try including the shortcut in the action name. For example, "Sharpen Photos (F7)" will always give you a reminder of what the shortcut key is.

Document Name: You can choose to have the original document name (in lower, upper, or title case) included in your file name.

Serial Number or Letter: You can also add an auto-incremented serial number or letter to the file name.

Date: You can add the date to the file name, as well, in several different formats.

Text: If you want to add your own custom text to the file name, just type into the field.

Extension: This adds the file extension to your name in lower or uppercase.

Compatibility: If you're creating files for the Web or you're moving them between a Mac and Windows, then it's best to check all options here.

ERRORS:
You have several choices when you run into errors when batch processing.

Stop For Errors: This will stop the batch process and notify you of each and every error. Realistically, it's not the best choice, since if there are errors you're better off choosing the next option, Log Errors To File, and reviewing them all at the end.

Log Errors To File: This logs all errors in a text file and allows the batch process to run all the way through. If you pick this option, then the Save As button will become enabled and you must pick a place for this error log text file to reside.

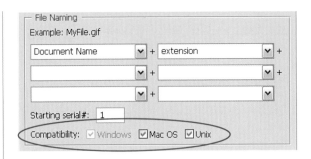

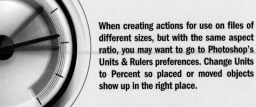

TURBO BOOST

When creating actions for use on files of different sizes, but with the same aspect ratio, you may want to go to Photoshop's Units & Rulers preferences. Change Units to Percent so placed or moved objects show up in the right place.

At this point, we've covered every setting there is when it comes to the Batch dialog. But I didn't want to stop there because I think it's important that you see how to use batch processing from start to finish.

BATCH PROCESSING FROM SCRATCH

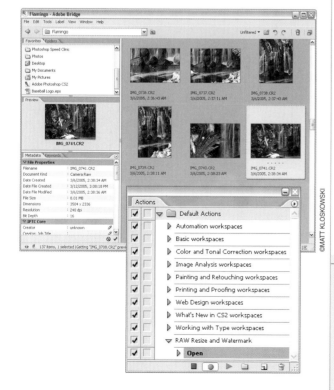

STEP ONE:
Okay, let's start from square one. First, we'll record an action to use for batch processing. In the Actions palette, click the Create New Action icon at the bottom of the palette. Name the action "RAW Resize and Watermark" and click Record to start recording the action.

STEP TWO:
Go into Bridge and find a RAW file. Double-click on the file to open it. When you see the Camera Raw dialog, just click Open to open the image in Photoshop. If you look in the Actions palette, you'll see that this step was recorded.

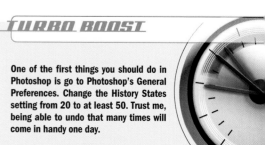

TURBO BOOST

One of the first things you should do in Photoshop is go to Photoshop's General Preferences. Change the History States setting from 20 to at least 50. Trust me, being able to undo that many times will come in handy one day.

Step Three:

Since we'll be adding a watermark, press Command-K (PC: Control-K) to go into Photoshop's Preferences. Choose Units & Rulers from the first pop-up menu. In the Units section, from the Rulers pop-up menu, select Percent. Click OK to save the changes and now everything you do in Photoshop will be done in percentages of the overall image dimensions and not actual pixel coordinates.

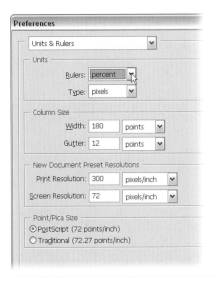

Step Four:

To resize this image for the Web, choose Image>Image Size. First, change the Resolution to 72 ppi and then change the Width to 640 pixels. Click OK.

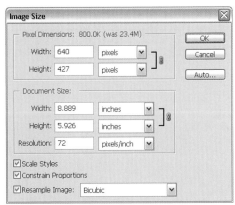

Step Five:

Press D to set your Foreground color to black. To create the watermark, select the Type tool (T), click on the photo (do not create a text box), and type your initials. I chose Myriad Bold at 150 pt for this example. Then click the Commit checkmark on the right side of the Options Bar. *Note:* I'm just using some simple letters here, but you could also use a logo or a shape for this watermark. Refer back to the tutorial on adding a watermark in Chapter 3 to see how to do this.

TURBO BOOST

Font previews are a great new feature. However, the preview size may be too small or too large for you. To change this setting, go into Photoshop's Preferences and choose Type. Adjust the Font Preview Size setting to your liking.

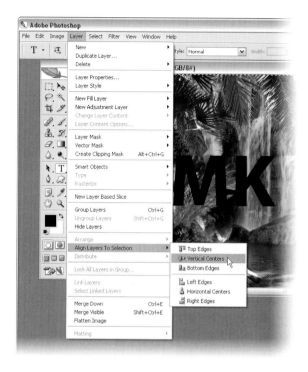

STEP SIX:

Next, to place the text in the exact center of the document, press Command-A (PC: Control-A) to Select All. Choose Layer>Align Layers To Selection>Vertical Centers. Then, choose Layer>Align Layers To Selection>Horizontal Centers. This will put the watermark in the exact center of the image no matter what the image dimensions are. Press Command-D (PC: Control-D) to Deselect.

STEP SEVEN:

Now, it's time to add the watermark style to this watermark. Double-click on the watermark layer to bring up the Layer Style dialog. Click on the Bevel and Emboss option on the left and leave the default settings.

TURBO BOOST

If you're always changing the Global Light settings in the Layer Style dialog to something other than the default, try this. With no document open, go to Layer>Layer Style>Global Light. Change the settings to create your own default.

STEP EIGHT:

Next, under Blending Options, in the Advanced Blending section, drop the Fill Opacity setting down to 0%. This should remove all of the color from the watermark but leave the beveled see-through appearance intact. Click OK to close the Layer Style dialog.

STEP NINE:

From the Layers palette's flyout menu, choose Flatten Image to flatten all layers.

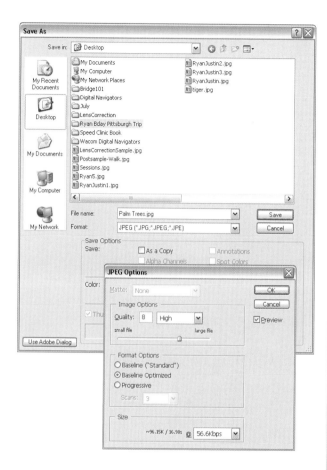

STEP TEN:

Save this image for the Web by choosing File>Save As. It doesn't matter at this point what you name the image because you're just recording the save settings—Batch will take care of the real naming for you later. In the Save As dialog, choose JPEG as the file format and click Save. The JPEG Options dialog will then open. Set the Quality to 8 with Baseline Optimized selected. Click OK to save the image.

STEP ELEVEN:

Okay, you're done with this part. Click the Stop Recording icon to stop recording the action.

TURBO BOOST

If you miss the old actions that used to ship with Photoshop (or just flat out don't like the workspace-related ones you see in the Actions palette), just go to the Actions palette's flyout menu and choose Sample Actions.

STEP TWELVE:

Now, let's batch an entire folder of images using this action. Open Bridge and select the images you want to batch. Then choose Tools>Photoshop>Batch.

STEP THIRTEEN:

From the Batch dialog, in the Play section, choose the set where you saved the RAW Resize and Watermark action that you just created. Then, from the Action pop-up menu, choose the action itself.

STEP FOURTEEN:

The Source setting will already be set to Bridge, so don't change that. However, make sure you check Override Action "Open" Commands and Suppress File Open Options Dialogs, so we don't see the Camera Raw window open each time.

TURBO BOOST

Another cool way to speed up batch processing actions is to go to Photoshop's Preferences and set the History States to 2, and click OK. Here's the catch—don't forget to change it back when you're done.

STEP FIFTEEN:

In the Destination section, select Folder and choose a folder on your Desktop (or anywhere on your computer) to save these images into. Check Override Action "Save As" Commands here, as well.

STEP SIXTEEN:

In the File Naming section, click once in the field that reads Document Name. Enter a name that is descriptive for these images, such as the location where they were taken. I'll use "Flamingo" for this example, since I shot these in the back of the Flamingo hotel. In the pop-up menu to the right, pick 3 Digit Serial Number and in the second pop-menu down on the left, choose extension. Also, make sure to enter "1" in the Starting Serial# field.

STEP SEVENTEEN:

Turn on all three Compatibility checkboxes to be sure these files will be compatible on both a Mac and a Windows PC.

TURBO BOOST

Instead of manually aligning type in a text box in your action, press Command-Shift-L (PC: Control-Shift-L) to left-align it. Substitute the L with a C for center-aligned type and an R for right alignment.

STEP EIGHTEEN:

In the Errors section, choose Log Errors To File. Click on Save As and select a folder in which to save the error log. Name it something descriptive like "Batch Errors" so it's easy to find later.

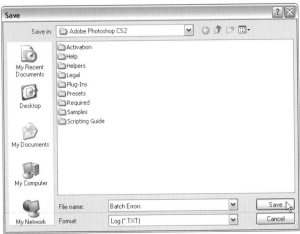

STEP NINETEEN:

Now, you're ready to run Batch. Just click OK to start. This is when you'll want to go get that cup of coffee, as this may take a while depending on how many images you've selected, but it's worth it. When Batch is done, go into Bridge and find the folder with your new images. If you open one in Photoshop, you'll see that they are indeed resized JPEG images with a water-mark on them and with the file name you chose. The best part is that Photoshop did all the work for you.

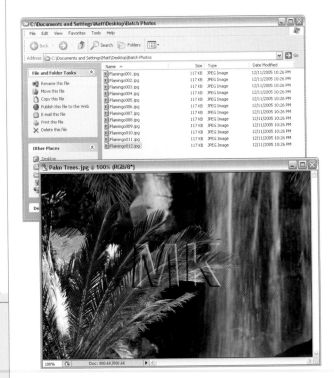

TURBO BOOST

You can't undo a recorded action step when you're actually recording the action. Photoshop will record an undo step instead. If you want to undo a step, stop recording the action and just drag the step to the Trash icon.

TURBO BOOST

If you ever make a selection and forget to
save it, just choose Select>Reselect.

CHAPTER 5

GET SMART

WORKING WITH SMART OBJECTS

I decided at the last minute to add a Smart Objects chapter to this book instead of the one tutorial that I had originally intended. Why? Because not only are Smart Objects a new feature in CS2, but they're an incredibly powerful and timesaving one as well. That's what this book is all about, right? Working faster and smarter in Photoshop. Smart Objects mark an entirely new way of thinking and working inside Photoshop and you'll be amazed at how much time and hassle they can save you. In a nutshell, this new feature is pure dynamite and I felt it deserved an entire chapter instead of just a few pages.

CREATING A SMART PICTURE PACKAGE

I have to tell you that one of my favorite things to demo in front of people is Photoshop CS2's new Smart Object feature. Imagine this: I create a custom picture package in Photoshop. I go on to insert multiple copies of a photo at different sizes in a document. Then I talk about changing the custom package to use another photo and how I need to go in and replace all of the photos manually. After that, I show how to do the same thing with Smart Objects with basically two clicks. The "ooooh" and "ahhhh" reactions that I get are priceless.

WHAT IS A SMART OBJECT AND WHY USE THEM?

I actually received this exact question from someone and I think it's a great place to start. Smart Objects allow you to non-destructively scale, transform, rotate, and warp any raster or vector graphic in Photoshop. The best part about them is the fact that Photoshop preserves the editability of the Smart Object layer no matter what, even for high-resolution vector graphics from Adobe Illustrator.

The results of enlarging an image that wasn't a Smart Object

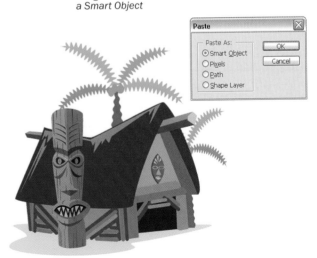

The same image enlarged as a Smart Object

TURBO BOOST

If you use the Place command in Photoshop (File>Place), Photoshop will automatically turn the placed image into a Smart Object for you.

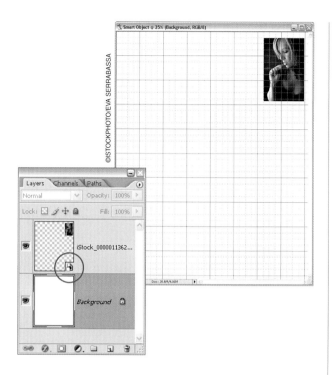

©ISTOCKPHOTO/EVA SERRABASSA

STEP ONE:

Choose File>New or press Command-N (PC: Control-N) to create a new blank document. From the Preset pop-up menu, choose 8x10 and then click OK. Turn on the grid by pressing Command-' (PC: Control-'), and turn on snapping by choosing View>Snap. Choose File>Place and navigate to a photo you want to add to the document. Click the Place button and your image will appear in the document. Press-and-hold the Shift key and adjust the bounding box around the photo to scale it down. Click-and-drag the photo toward the top-right corner and press the Return (PC: Enter) key to confirm the placed image. You can tell it was placed as a Smart Object because you'll see a small icon in the bottom-right corner of the layer thumbnail in the Layers palette.

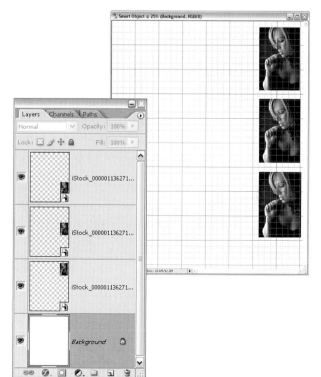

STEP TWO:

Duplicate that layer two times by pressing Command-J (PC: Control-J). Then, click on the first layer copy and use the Move tool (V) to place it below the original along the right side of the document. Repeat this with the second layer copy.

TURBO BOOST

Instead of always using the Layer menu, most of the Smart Object commands can be accessed from a pop-up menu by Control-clicking (PC: Right-clicking) on the name of a Smart Object within the Layers palette.

STEP THREE:

Duplicate the layer a third time. This time, press Command-T (PC: Control-T) to go into Free Transform mode. Press-and-hold the Shift key while you click-and-drag a corner point to make this copy larger. Place it on the left side of the layout and press Return (PC: Enter). Notice how the quality of the photo is retained, even though we resized it. If this weren't a Smart Object, increasing the size of the photo would cause it to lose quality.

STEP FOUR:

That's not it, though. Resizing and transforming Smart Objects without losing quality is cool enough, but there's another little trick you can do. Let's say you want to change the photo and create another custom picture package. Try this: First, press Command-' (PC: Control-') to turn off the grid. Click on one of the Smart Object layers and choose Layer>Smart Objects>Replace Contents. This will open the Place dialog again. Just go find another photo and click Place. Magically (okay, maybe not) all of the photos will be replaced with the new photo and you'll automatically have another custom picture package.

TURBO BOOST

Press Command-0 (PC: Control-0) while using Free Transform to quickly zoom out and see any handles that are beyond the visible image area.

©ISTOCKPHOTO/EVA SERRABASSA

In the previous tutorial, you saw how you can easily replace a Smart Object. However, what happens if you don't want to replace all of the Smart Objects? Maybe you only want to change some or one of them. Sometimes Smart Objects are too smart for their own good, but there are ways to work around them and get the results you want.

REPLACING ONLY ONE SMART OBJECT

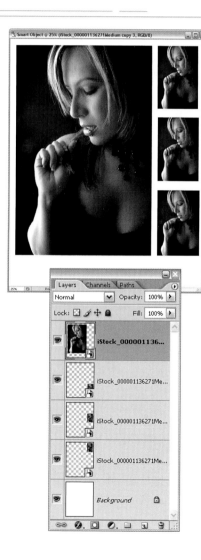

STEP ONE:

Follow Steps One through Three in the previous tutorial to create a custom picture package. You should wind up with a document with four Smart Objects in it, each of the same photo.

TURBO BOOST

When editing a Smart Object, don't choose File>Save As since it will save a file on your hard drive independent of the Smart Object. That will prevent the changes from being reflected in the Smart Object since they were never saved back to the original document.

STEP TWO:

Now, let's say you want to replace only one of the photos (the large one, in this example) but leave the other ones as is. Click once on the layer with the large photo to target it. Choose Group into New Smart Object from the Layers palette's fly-out menu. You won't see anything change here, but you've essentially broken the link between this Smart Object and the others that you created it from.

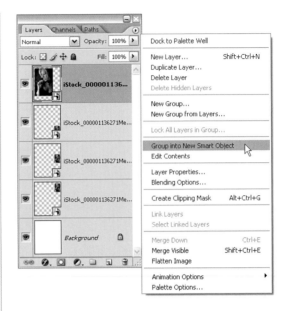

STEP THREE:

Now, on the same layer, choose Layer> Smart Objects>Replace Contents. Navigate to another photo in the Place dialog and click the Place button. This time, only the large photo on the left is changed and the other three photos on the right remain the same. This happens because in Step Two we grouped this layer into a new Smart Object, making it an independent Smart Object, not just a duplicate of the original.

Choose Layer>Smart Objects>Convert to Layer in order to apply filters, gradients, or brush strokes to a Smart Object layer. However, keep in mind that the layer will no longer be a Smart Object.

One thing that many people don't realize is that Smart Objects aren't restricted to regular JPEG photos or vector artwork. You can actually place a Camera Raw file as a Smart Object. Now, why the heck would you want to do this? Well, let's say you decide you'd like to reprocess the Camera Raw file once it's inside a Photoshop document. If it's a Smart Object, you can go back and edit the original RAW settings at any point.

SMART OBJECTS AND CAMERA RAW

STEP ONE:
Open an image that you'd like to work with. Here, I've used a file with a blue background. Choose File>Place. This time, instead of placing a regular old JPEG photo, select a RAW photo and press the Place button. The Camera Raw dialog will open so you can process your RAW photo (I've done a few adjustments and some cropping here). When you're done, press Open to place the photo into Photoshop. Just position it where you want and press the Return (PC: Enter) key. (I've also added a Stroke and Outer Glow layer style to the photo here.)

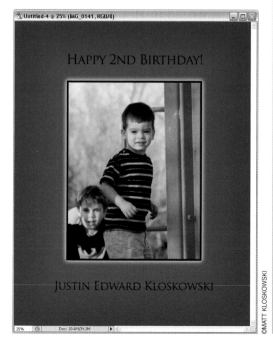

TURBO BOOST

When you double-click a Smart Object layer's thumbnail to edit it, you'll probably see a warning dialog telling you to make sure you use File>Save to save changes. Go ahead and check Don't Show Again in this dialog, so it doesn't continue interrupting you.

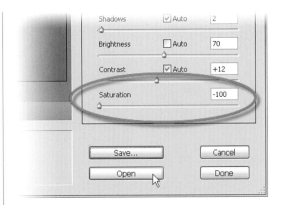

STEP TWO:

Now, let's say you continue to work on this design and later realize that you need to adjust the photo more. Since it's a Smart Object, just double-click on the layer thumbnail and the Camera Raw dialog will open again. It'll be populated with the settings you used before and you can change them here. When you're done, just click the Open button again and Photoshop will update the photo to reflect the changes you just made.

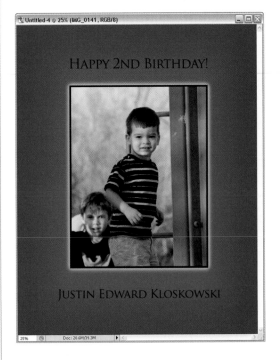

TURBO BOOST

You can actually change the opacity of an image as you're placing it before committing the place. I know it sounds weird, but make sure you type the percentage in the Layers palette to change it. This won't work with the sliders.

Truth be told, I'm a big Illustrator user. I usually use Photoshop and Illustrator together almost every day. I often create vector artwork in Illustrator, paste it into Photoshop, and inevitably want to change the artwork. So, I'd change the artwork in Illustrator and re-paste it into Photoshop. As you can imagine, this process is slow. With Smart Objects, it's a lot easier. I insert the artwork as a Smart Object and Photoshop links back to the original file for editing and automatic updating.

WORKING WITH SMART OBJECTS IN PHOTOSHOP AND ILLUSTRATOR

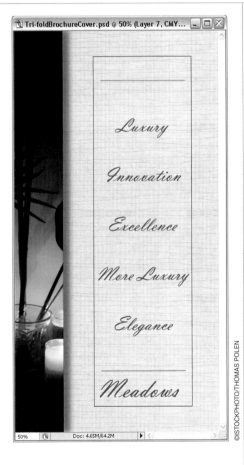

©ISTOCKPHOTO/THOMAS POLEN

STEP ONE:
A great candidate for a Smart Object is a logo. Typically, logos are vector files created in Illustrator. If you were to simply copy-and-paste the logo from Illustrator into Photoshop, then every time the logo changed you'd need to re-paste it into Photoshop. Smart Objects make this process a lot easier. First, open a design in Photoshop that you'd like to insert an Illustrator file into.

TURBO BOOST

Remember that vector Smart Objects work the same as rasterized ones. In the first tutorial in this chapter, you replaced multiple instances of the photo with another one. The same thing holds true for vector Smart Objects, as well.

STEP TWO:

Now choose File>Place. Find the logo on your hard disk and click Place. You'll then see another Place dialog where you can just press OK to select the defaults.

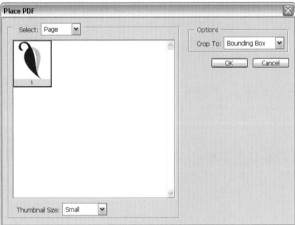

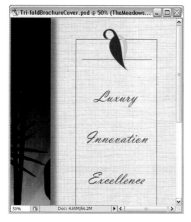

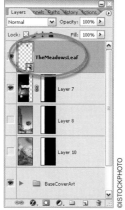

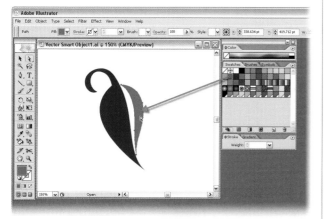

STEP THREE:

Next, you'll see the logo appear with a bounding box around it on your image. You can resize it as needed (remember it's a vector graphic so you can make it as large as you want) and move it into place. Press the Return (PC: Enter) key when you're done and you'll have placed the vector file into your image as a Smart Object.

STEP FOUR:

Now, let's hypothetically imagine that a client requests a change to the logo (you know how those clients can be, right?). It could be simple or it could be complicated, but let's stick with a simple color change here. Since you placed the logo as a Smart Object, just double-click on the Smart Object layer's thumbnail and Illustrator will launch (if it's not open already). The logo will open inside of it because Photoshop knows that this is the default editing application for vector files. Now, using the Direct Selection tool (A), click on one part of the logo and change its fill color to a light green.

STEP FIVE:

Choose File>Save (or just press Command-S [PC: Control-S]) and Illustrator will save the changes. That's not all, though. If you switch back to Photoshop, you'll see that the changes are automatically reflected in your document without you having to re-paste or replace anything.

TURBO BOOST

You can't paint on a Smart Object layer but you can cheat a little. Create a new empty layer above the Smart Object and choose Layer>Create Clipping Mask. Now, anything painted on the empty layer will only appear on the Smart Object where there are pixels.

WARP, TWIST, TURN, DISTORT, AND TRANSFORM ANYTHING NON-DESTRUCTIVELY

When Adobe released Photoshop CS2, they included a new feature called Warp that was really a big hit. With this feature, you can bend, twist, and transform images in ways that were never before possible. However, once you warp an image, it is warped forever. If you close the file, then you can never get it back the way it used to be. Not so with Smart Objects. Smart Objects are infinitely changeable and you can always go back and edit those changes (or even take them away) if you want.

STEP ONE:

Create a new blank file with a white background. Choose File>Place to place a photo into this layout and resize it to fit the page. Press Return (PC: Enter) when you are done. You should be left with a white background layer and a photo as a Smart Object on top of it.

TURBO BOOST

There is no keyboard shortcut for Warp. But if you press Command-T (PC: Control-T) to go into Free Transform and click the icon in the Options Bar (just to the left of the Cancel icon), you can toggle between the two modes.

STEP TWO:

In this example, let's create a page curl effect with this photo using Photoshop CS2's new Warp feature. Choose Edit>Transform>Warp. You'll see a grid appear over your image letting you know you're ready to warp.

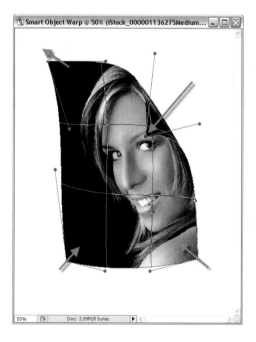

STEP THREE:

Each point on this grid can be moved and manipulated for a realistic warping effect. In this example, grab the top-right handle and drag it toward the bottom left to create a page curling effect. As a little side note here, if you drag it far enough you'll actually start to see the underside of the photo—cool, huh? Anyway, back to the matter at hand. After you've dragged the corner point, you can move the other corners around just to give the appearance that the photo is curling. Press the Return (PC: Enter) key when you're done to commit the warp.

TURBO BOOST

If you decide to re-edit a warp in a Smart Object (by returning to Warp mode), you could choose None from the Warp pop-up menu and the photo will go back to normal. Now that's working smarter, not harder.

Okay, this really isn't a Speed Bump, but I had to get your attention. The designer in me can't let you continue without suggesting to add a Drop Shadow layer style behind this photo (yep, you can even add layer styles to Smart Object layers). Okay, now you can go back and finish the tutorial.

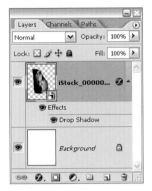

STEP FOUR:

Normally, if this were anything but a Smart Object, you'd be stuck with this warp even if you wanted to change it. However, since you converted this to a Smart Object first, you can choose Edit>Transform>Warp once again, and you'll see that Photoshop remembered your warp settings. You can choose None from the Warp pop-up menu in the Options Bar to reset the Smart Object or you can just tweak the warp grid if you want. Either way, think of the possibilities you now have because of the non-destructive nature of Smart Objects.

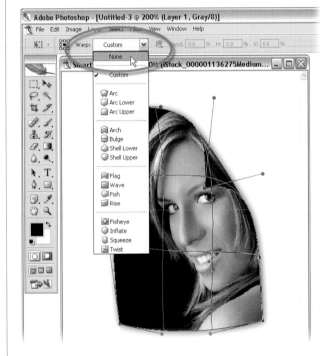

TURBO BOOST

Perspective and Distort aren't available under Edit>Transform with Smart Objects. Instead, in Warp mode, choose Arc from the Warp pop-up menu in the Options Bar. Lower the Bend to 0%, and increase the Height to fake a perspective.

TURBO BOOST

While in Warp mode, you can press Command-T (PC: Control-T) to quickly switch to Free Transform. Unfortunately, pressing Command-T again doesn't switch back to Warp mode.

CHAPTER 6

SPEEDING UP THE RAW WORKFLOW

SEE HOW YOU CAN MAKE CAMERA RAW FLY!

I'm going to start here by doing something that is not done anywhere else in this book. Yep, I'm being rebellious. I'm breaking the mold. I'm rocking the boat. I'm...okay, you get the point. Now that I've built all of this suspense, what could I possibly be talking about? Well, I'm going to give you a tip right here in the chapter introduction. The tip is, if you don't shoot in RAW format, then don't read this chapter. It will not help you. In fact it may even hurt you. Okay, it won't really hurt you, but don't read it because it doesn't affect you. Now, if you're reading on then you'll probably relate to the fact that we've all heard a photographer here or there talk about the time involved in processing files in Camera Raw. Well, that has all changed in CS2. Adobe included a bunch of new features that dramatically speed up the work that you do in Camera Raw. I mean it. If you shoot in RAW or are thinking about it, then this chapter will save you time.

OPENING PHOTOS IN ADOBE CAMERA RAW (ACR)

When I first started using Photoshop CS2 it was a little confusing with all the different ways there were to open a RAW photo in ACR. (By the way, ACR is simply an easier "techie" way to say Adobe Camera Raw—there, don't you feel better now?) You can open a photo in Camera Raw from Adobe Bridge. But did you know there are two Camera Raws: one in Photoshop and one in Bridge? Or that you can open a RAW photo from Photoshop into Camera Raw or you can bypass Camera Raw altogether, etc.? So, I thought I'd give a quick recap (a recap I wish I had when I started) of all the ways to open a RAW photo.

THE DIFFERENCE BETWEEN BRIDGE'S CAMERA RAW AND PHOTOSHOP'S CAMERA RAW:

Okay, before we even talk about the different ways to open a RAW file, you first need to realize that you can open a photo in Camera Raw from Bridge or from Photoshop—each one is different. If you open a photo in Bridge's Camera Raw, you can't use Bridge in the background but you can use Photoshop. If you open a photo in Photoshop's Camera Raw, you can't use Photoshop but you can still use Bridge. Keep in mind, though, that both versions of Camera Raw are essentially the same and neither has more features than the other. Now that we have that down, let's see all the different ways to do it.

METHOD ONE:

The most intuitive method is to open a RAW file from Photoshop's Open dialog. When you do this, the RAW file opens in Photoshop's version of Camera Raw. You can edit away in it then, but you won't be able to get back to Photoshop until you dismiss the Camera Raw dialog by pressing

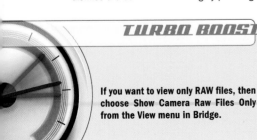

If you want to view only RAW files, then choose Show Camera Raw Files Only from the View menu in Bridge.

©MATT KLOSKOWSKI

one of the buttons at the bottom. Save will let you save the photo into another format such as TIF, JPEG, PSD, or DNG (digital negative format). Pressing Open will open the RAW photo in Photoshop with your current Camera Raw settings applied. Done will just close the Camera Raw dialog, saving your edits to the photo and returning you to Photoshop. Finally, Cancel does just what is says—it closes the dialog and cancels any editing you've done to the RAW file, as well as returning you to Photoshop.

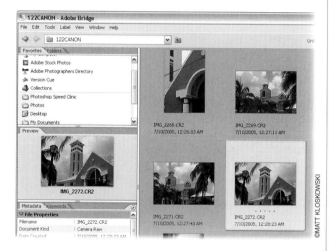

METHOD TWO:

The next method is inside Bridge. If you just double-click a RAW file in Bridge, you'll launch the Camera Raw dialog in Photoshop and the same rules as Method One apply.

©MATT KLOSKOWSKI

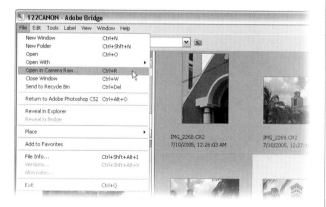

METHOD THREE:

The other Bridge-based way of opening a RAW file is by choosing File>Open in Camera Raw (or pressing Command-R [PC: Control-R]). You can Command-click (PC: Right-click) on an image to open it this way, as well. This is actually the one I use most because it opens the RAW file in Bridge's version of Camera Raw. This leaves me free to work in Photoshop while Camera Raw is processing my files in the background.

TURBO BOOST

To select all images for editing in Camera Raw, just press Command-A (PC: Control-A).

Method Four:

This last method is useful when you just want to open a photo with the current ACR settings applied to it and bypass the Camera Raw dialog altogether. In Bridge, just press-and-hold the Shift key and double-click on the RAW file. The current Camera Raw settings will automatically be applied to the photo and it will open directly in Photoshop, bypassing the Camera Raw dialog altogether.

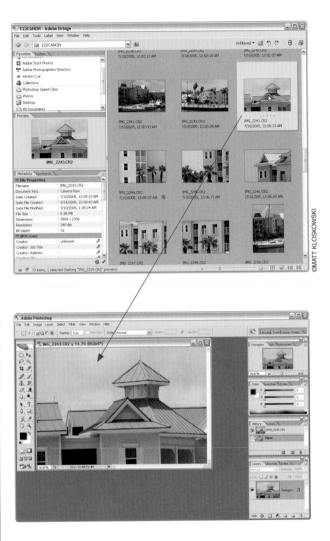

©MATT KLOSKOWSKI

TURBO BOOST

Toggle Camera Raw's Auto adjustments on and off by pressing Command-U (PC: Control-U).

Sometimes I use Camera Raw to create black-and-white photos. Since this conversion has a few steps (such as setting the Saturation to 0), it's a good candidate to save the settings to reapply to other photos. Here's the problem: By just using the Save Settings option, Camera Raw saves everything (exposure, contrast, etc.) and that's not good since each photo's ideal settings may be different. I only want to save a few settings. That's where Save Settings Subset comes in handy. It lets me just save a subset of the settings I want and leave the rest alone.

SAVING SPECIFIC SETTINGS IN CAMERA RAW

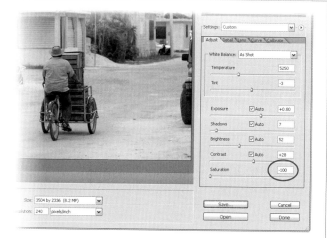

STEP ONE:
Open a photo in Camera Raw that you'd like to convert to black and white. In the Adjust tab, the first thing you'll need to do is click-and-drag the Saturation slider all the way to the left and drop it down to -100.

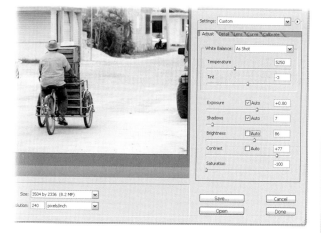

STEP TWO:
Next, you may also want to adjust the Contrast or Brightness, as well as any other settings under the Adjust tab, for this specific photo. However, those settings will most likely differ for each black-and-white conversion while the Saturation change is likely one that will always be the same.

TURBO BOOST

If you want to quickly see if your Camera Raw adjustments have helped or hurt your current photo, just press the P key to toggle the Preview checkbox at the top of the window on and off.

STEP THREE:

Now, go under the Calibrate tab. Here you can adjust the Red, Green, and Blue channels to really enhance the black-and-white effect. Again, these settings may change for each photo but you'll probably develop a few favorites here, so why not save them as well?

THE PROBLEM:

If you click the small, right-facing triangle next to the Settings pop-up menu, you'll see two Save Settings options on the resulting flyout menu—one for Save Settings and another for Save Settings Subset. If I were to choose the Save Settings option, Camera Raw would save all of the settings, not just the Saturation and those under the Calibrate tab. That would be fine if every photo looked the same, but they don't. It's likely that each photo you take will require different Exposure, Contrast, and Brightness settings, so we probably don't want to save those. Here's what to do to avoid that.

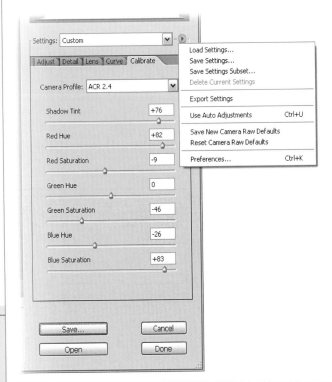

TURBO BOOST

Press-and-hold the Option (PC: Alt) key when manipulating the Exposure and Shadow sliders to see highlight and shadow clipping.

STEP FOUR:

Choose Save Settings Subset from the flyout menu that appears when you click that small triangle. You'll see the dialog on the left appear.

STEP FIVE:

Since you don't want to save anything else besides Saturation and Calibration settings, uncheck everything except the Saturation and Calibration options. Click Save to save these settings. Name it something descriptive like "Black and White Conversion" because this saved setting is going to show up in your Settings menu when you're done and you want to be able to find it quickly later on. Click the Save button when you're done.

STEP SIX:

To use this custom setting, just open another photo in Camera Raw. Click on the Settings pop-up menu, select the black-and-white custom setting subset you just created, and your black-and-white Saturation and Calibration settings will automatically be applied.

TURBO BOOST

When you're working with RAW files in Bridge, you can press Command-Option-C (PC: Control-Alt-C) to copy Camera Raw settings from one file and press Command-Option-V (PC: Control-Alt-V) to paste those same settings to another file.

©MATT KLOSKOWSKI

MAKING CHANGES TO MULTIPLE RAW FILES AT ONCE

Recently, on a trip to Tokyo, I was shooting some nighttime scenery and set my white balance to Cloudy. The next day, I went out on a photo shoot and shot a bunch of photos in perfect daylight using the same white balance setting—not good. Normally, that might be a problem, but with Camera Raw in Photoshop CS2, it's an easy fix.

STEP ONE:

In Bridge, navigate to the photos that you'd like to edit. Select one photo, then Command-click (PC: Control-click) on several other photos to add them to the selection.

STEP TWO:

Press the Return (PC: Enter) key to open these files in Camera Raw. The dialog will open showing the first photo (from Bridge) in the main preview area. However, if you look over to the left side, you'll see the other photos you opened, as well.

TURBO BOOST

Toggle the clipping warning checkboxes (at the top right of the image preview) on and off with their keyboard shortcuts instead. Use U for Shadows and O for Highlights.

©MATT KLOSKOWSKI

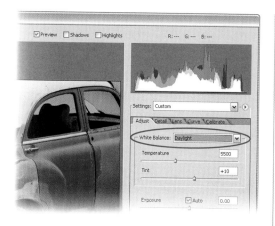

STEP THREE:

Don't do anything different yet. Just edit your photo as you normally would. In this case, I changed the White Balance setting from Cloudy to Daylight. This changes only the currently selected photo that is open in the main preview area.

STEP FOUR:

To apply this edit to the rest of the photos, look in the top-left corner of the screen and click the Select All button. All of the photos along the left will then be selected for editing.

STEP FIVE:

Now click the Synchronize button. You'll see the Synchronize dialog open. Make sure that any setting changes you've made are checked here (in this case, White Balance). Click OK and Camera Raw will apply the same changes to all of the photos at once. That's all there is to it!

TURBO BOOST

When using the Synchronize option in Camera Raw (with multiple images open), press-and-hold the Option (PC: Alt) key to bypass the Synchronize dialog and apply the last setting used.

STRAIGHTENING CROOKED PHOTOS IN CAMERA RAW

Ever try straightening a crooked photo in Photoshop? Honestly, I've always thought it was kind of a pain in the neck. It involves using the Measure tool, remembering angles, arbitrary rotating, and cropping, and...well, you get the picture. That's why I was so psyched when the Straighten tool came about in Camera Raw 3 (with Photoshop CS2). It not only straightens the photo very quickly, but it also crops it to maintain the maximum rectangular size of the image. It saves me so much time and it's a lot easier to use.

STEP ONE:
Go ahead and open a photo in Camera Raw. As you look across Camera Raw's Toolbox at the top, you'll see the familiar Crop tool icon. Just to the right of that is the new Straighten tool (A). Click once on the tool to select it.

STEP TWO:
Drag the tool along an area in the photo that should be horizontal or vertical. In this example, I'm just dragging across the horizon line.

TURBO BOOST

Use the Straighten tool in Camera Raw to automatically straighten your photos before you even get into Photoshop.

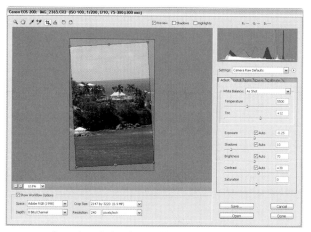

Even though the photo still looks crooked, it will be straightened when opened in Photoshop

STEP THREE:
The Camera Raw preview window will update to show you the cropped rectangle. Keep in mind, though, you'll continue to see only the uncropped, unstraightened version of the photo in Camera Raw.

STEP FOUR:
Press Open to open this image in Photoshop. At this point, Photoshop will show the straightened and cropped photo.

A lot of people get confused because Camera Raw doesn't actually remove the crop area of the photo from view. Don't forget that once you apply a crop or straighten to a photo, even though the Camera Raw preview doesn't show you the results, the settings are indeed saved and will update in the photo's preview in Bridge.

TURBO BOOST

In Camera Raw, when using the Crop tool try pressing the Caps Lock key to switch the cursor to a crosshair. This makes it easier to see the cursor when cropping.

SAVING MULTIPLE PHOTOS IN THE BACKGROUND

One thing I never liked about the previous version of Camera Raw was that working with multiple files at the same time just wasn't possible. If editing each individual photo wasn't enough of a pain, imagine saving 15 or 20 8-megapixel RAW files one at a time. It was time consuming and tedious. Now, in the latest version of Camera Raw, not only can I open multiple photos at once in the Camera Raw dialog and apply my settings to them, but I can also save them all at once. Even better, I can save them as a background process so I can still work while they're saving.

STEP ONE:

This trick really works best when you're using Camera Raw in Bridge instead of Photoshop. Mainly because its benefits come from the fact that you can still work in Photoshop while your photos are saving in the background. So, in Bridge select a bunch of RAW photos to open. Then press Command-R (PC: Control-R) to open the photos in Bridge's Camera Raw.

STEP TWO:

Once Camera Raw opens, you'll see the first photo in the preview window, but you'll also see the others along the left side of the dialog. Go ahead and make your adjustments to the photos as you normally would. When you're done and you're ready to save the photos (yep, all of them at the same time) just press the Select All button at the top left of the dialog.

TURBO BOOST

Don't forget to turn on the Shadows and Highlights checkboxes at the top of the Camera Raw dialog to visually see if you're clipping any highlights or shadows when you make adjustments.

©MATT KLOSKOWSKI

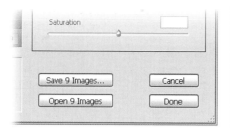

STEP THREE:

After the photos are selected, click the Save Images button at the bottom right of the dialog. Now you'll see the Save Options dialog open.

STEP FOUR:

Starting from the top, choose the Destination where you want to save your images. You can save them in the same location, or choose a new location by choosing Save in New Location from the pop-up menu or pressing the Select Folder button.

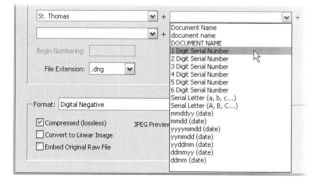

STEP FIVE:

Next, you can choose how you want to name the files. Usually, I name them something descriptive from when or where I took the photos. You can also add serial numbers, serial letters, or a date to your images using the pop-up menus.

While in the Camera Raw dialog, press Command-K (PC: Control-K) to view Camera Raw Preferences.

STEP SIX:

The File Extension setting is probably the most important here. You'll need to decide what format you want to save these photos in. For this example, we're going to use JPEG. When you change this in Windows, you'll notice the Format section below automatically updates with options relating to whatever format you chose. I'm leaving the Quality setting at 8 here. On a Mac, you'll first need to choose the file format from the Format pop-up menu. Then you can choose the File Extension setting.

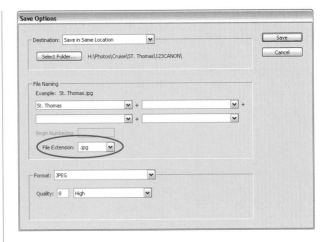

STEP SEVEN:

Okay, here's the cool part. Finally, you're ready to save the photos, so just press the Save button. The dialog will close and you'll be returned to the Camera Raw dialog. If you look directly above the four buttons at the bottom right of the dialog, you'll see a message indicating the progress of the photos being saved. What's really great is that you can now continue to edit other photos while Camera Raw is processing your photos in the background. Cool, huh?

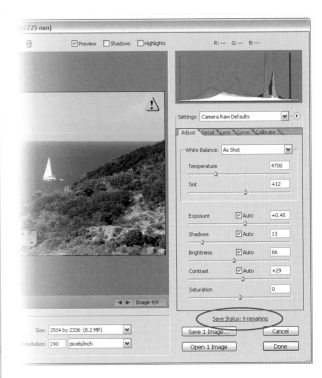

TURBO BOOST

When saving files in the background you can even close the Camera Raw dialog. Go into Bridge and open other files. When you do this, you'll see that the progress still displays in the Camera Raw Save Status dialog.

I was trying out some product photography techniques one day, so I set my camera on a tripod and pointed at the same product for about 20 minutes. I experimented with a bunch of different exposure, white balance, and aperture settings. When I was done, I had a lot of the same photos and I realized they all needed to be cropped. That's where the ability to crop multiple photos in Camera Raw saved the day.

CROPPING MULTIPLE PHOTOS AT THE SAME TIME

©MATT KLOSKOWSKI

STEP ONE:
Open several RAW photos that all need to be cropped. This works best if the photos are of the same subject at the same focal length, since customizing the crop for each individual photo somewhat defeats the speed aspect of this tutorial. As you can see here, these photos all show part of the background beyond the backdrop, so they can definitely benefit from cropping.

STEP TWO:
Select the Crop tool (C) in Camera Raw's Toolbox. Click-and-drag with the Crop tool just as you normally would when using it in Photoshop. When you release the mouse button, you'll see a crop area around your photo. The area that you cropped won't be removed, though. It's still there—remember, this is a RAW file so your changes aren't permanent. You will, however, see a preview of the cropped photo in the images on the left side of the dialog.

TURBO BOOST

When using Curve in Camera Raw, hold down the Command (PC: Control) key and hover over an area in the image. You'll see a small circle appear on the curve indicating which brightness values will be affected by adjusting the curve.

STEP THREE:

To apply the crop to multiple photos, just press the Select All button to select all photos in Camera Raw. Then press Synchronize and you'll see the Synchronize dialog appear. The most important thing to do here is to turn on the Crop checkbox. If you've made other changes to the first photo here that you want applied to all photos, then select those settings as well. Press OK to actually apply the Synchronize settings.

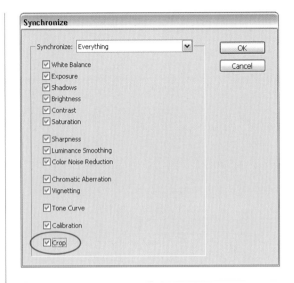

STEP FOUR:

You'll see all the photos update on the left side of the dialog. Visually you can see that they were cropped, but you can also look for the small Crop icon next to each one to verify. At this point, you can open these photos in Photoshop, or just press Done and Camera Raw will save your changes. If you open any of these photos again in Camera Raw, you'll still see the cropping border right where you left it.

TURBO BOOST

Add a point to the curve in Camera Raw by Command-clicking (PC: Control-clicking) on the image. You can then use the Up Arrow and Down Arrow keys to adjust that point on the curve.

A buddy of mine called me up panicked one day after a photo shoot. He was a great photographer, but just getting into this "digital thing," as he called it. He had just finished shooting an entire day in a color space (on his camera) he didn't even know existed. His local printer always required him to send his files in the sRGB color space, and he was worried that this would be a problem. Luckily, he shot in RAW mode, so it doesn't matter what color profile he assigned in the camera during shooting because you can just assign the proper profile in Camera Raw later.

ASSIGNING CAMERA PROFILES OUTSIDE OF THE CAMERA

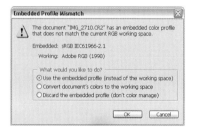

©MATT KLOSKOWSKI

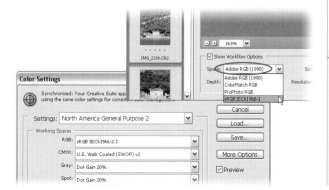

ABOUT COLOR PROFILES IN Camera Raw:

The color profile is the one that your image will be converted to when it actually opens into Photoshop. It doesn't have to be the same as what you selected in your camera when you shot it, since a RAW image really doesn't have a color space until it is converted.

STEP ONE:

Open any RAW photos that need the color profile changed. Press the Select All button at the top left of the Camera Raw dialog. This will select all photos for editing and any changes you make will now affect all of them.

STEP TWO:

Look for the Space setting down near the Workflow Options area in this window. Notice how the Space setting reads Adobe RGB (1998). Change this to sRGB IEC61966-1. That's it! The change will be applied to all of the photos you have open in Camera Raw. Just click the Done button, and now when any of those photos are opened in Photoshop they'll use the sRGB color profile instead of Adobe RGB. Just choose Edit>Color Settings to see for yourself.

TURBO BOOST

When you're using Curve in Camera Raw you can press Control-Tab (on both a Mac and a PC) to cycle through the points on the curve so you can edit them.

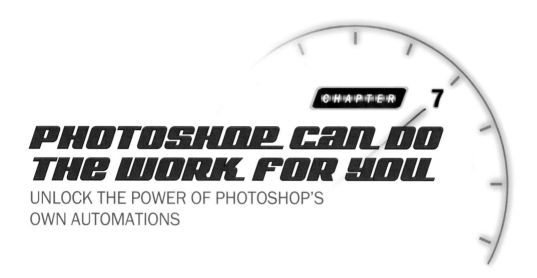

CHAPTER 7

PHOTOSHOP CAN DO THE WORK FOR YOU

UNLOCK THE POWER OF PHOTOSHOP'S OWN AUTOMATIONS

This chapter is all about letting Photoshop do the work for you. You'd be amazed at just how many little gems lie in the Automation menu in Photoshop and, for that matter, Bridge as well. The problem with some of these automations is that they're sometimes a little too hidden or too tricky to use. That's where this chapter comes in. We'll take a look at most of the automations in Photoshop and how to use them. Along the way, I'll show you some of the key settings, including which ones can make your life easier and which ones can slow you down.

BRIDGE OR PHOTOSHOP? READ THIS BEFORE YOU BEGIN THIS CHAPTER

A lot of people ask me why the Tools menu in Adobe Bridge (Tools>Photoshop) contains many of the same automations and tasks that the Automate menu has in Photoshop (File>Automate). The first thing I tell them is that I have absolutely no idea why (sorry, I have to be truthful). However, just so I don't leave them hanging, I follow that answer up with my explanation of what is different between the two options and which one I prefer most.

BACKGROUND:

You can run Photoshop automations in two different ways. I'm going to give you what I think is the fastest way and I'll tell you why. First, be aware that regardless of which method you use, the automations we'll cover here all run from within Photoshop and require Photoshop to be open. It's just the process of starting them that is different.

METHOD ONE: PHOTOSHOP

The first way to run automations is probably the one you're most familiar with. In Photoshop, if you choose File>Automate you'll see a bunch of different automations that you can run on your images. In most cases, one of the first steps in each automation is picking the source images. Generally, you'll see a choice of using all open files, a folder, or images from Bridge (which will be grayed out if you're running it from Photoshop). Now, there's nothing wrong with running these automations from Photoshop and I'll admit it is convenient since you're probably already working in Photoshop. However, I urge you to read on to Method Two, since that is my preferred way and the one that I'll be using throughout this chapter.

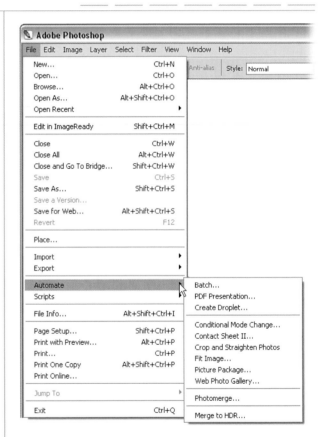

TURBO BOOST

Automations aren't just limited to Photoshop. Under the Tools menu in Bridge, you'll see there are options for Illustrator and InDesign.

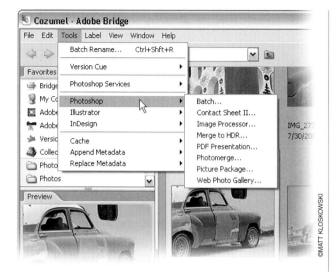

©MATT KLOSKOWSKI

METHOD TWO: BRIDGE

This method is actually the one that I suggest and will be using for the tutorials in this chapter. In Bridge, if you look under the Tools>Photoshop menu you'll see a bunch of Photoshop automations. The way this works is that you select the images you want to work with, and then choose the automation from the Tools>Photoshop menu. Now, you may ask why I like this method the best. I like it because I can choose my images visually before I run the automation. If you were to run this from Photoshop you'd have to either open all of the images you wanted to work with or choose them by file name or folder (none of which is really useful or fast, and remember this book is about doing things smarter and faster). The other cool thing about running automations from Bridge is that you can do a search that brings back images from multiple folders all over your computer. That way, if you wanted to run an automation on specific images it's really easy to do.

TURBO BOOST

If you want to remove Camera Raw adjustments in Bridge without going back into Camera Raw, just select the image and choose Edit>Apply Camera Raw Settings>Clear Camera Raw Settings.

CROP AND STRAIGHTEN

One day I received a question from a National Association of Photoshop Professionals (NAPP) member. He asked if there was a better way to crop large numbers of photos that he'd scanned. He went on to explain how he'd spent hours gang scanning photos into his computer and then cropping each one individually in Photoshop. To his surprise, I replied that this could be done with an automation that was already built right into Photoshop.

STEP ONE:

Place multiple images on your scanner and scan them into your computer. The Crop and Straighten Photos automation will tend to work best on photos with clearly defined edges, so keep that in mind. When you scan them, you should get a single file with multiple photos in it.

©CARLINE ZUMBANO

TURBO BOOST

If the Crop and Straighten Photos automation incorrectly splits one of your photos, make a selection of the image and some background, then press-and-hold the Option (PC: Alt) key when you choose the automation to separate only one image.

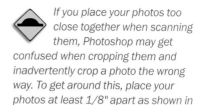

If you place your photos too close together when scanning them, Photoshop may get confused when cropping them and inadvertently crop a photo the wrong way. To get around this, place your photos at least 1/8" apart as shown in Step One.

STEP TWO:
Open the scanned image in Photoshop. I know I said we were going to use Bridge in this chapter, but this is one of the few automations that isn't included in Bridge (again, I have no idea why) so you'll have to use Photoshop here. Now, you can use this feature in one of two ways. First, you can draw a selection around the images that you want to crop and straighten and Photoshop will only use the photos in that selection area. Or you can just use an entire layer, which is what I use the most. Then, from the File menu choose Automate>Crop and Straighten Photos. The automation will start processing your photos and placing each one in its own window.

TURBO BOOST

The Crop and Straighten Photos automation will still work even if you just have one scanned photo. It's a nice way to quickly straighten it after the fact, so you don't have to try to get it perfect while scanning.

CREATING A PDF PRESENTATION FOR YOUR CLIENTS, FRIENDS, OR FAMILY

Creating a PDF Presentation is a great way to get your work in front of clients, friends, or family. What's nice about sending your work this way is you have total control over the presentation of your images. You can set up the PDF to open as a slide show presentation with transitions and everything, or just open as a regular PDF. Even better is the fact that you can control security settings, so if want to send a high-quality PDF but don't want anyone printing your work without paying for it first, that's no problem.

STEP ONE:

In Bridge, select the images that you want to include in the PDF Presentation. From the Tools menu, choose Photoshop>PDF Presentation. Photoshop will open, along with the PDF Presentation dialog. Here, you'll be able to add, duplicate, or remove any images, if you'd like. The presentation will show the images as they are listed, from top to bottom in this dialog. You can change the order in which the images appear by clicking-and-dragging the names up or down in the Source Files section.

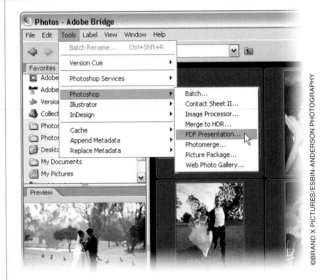

©BRAND X PICTURES/ESBIN-ANDERSON PHOTOGRAPHY

Since you can't see the actual images in the Source Files section, it'll be difficult to determine which is which in case you want to change the display order. It's best to move the images in the order you want in Bridge before you even run this automation, so you can see them visually.

TURBO BOOST

Don't forget that you can view PDF files in Bridge's Preview palette. You can also page through them in Slide Show mode, too. Just press the Left and Right Arrow keys to page through the PDF.

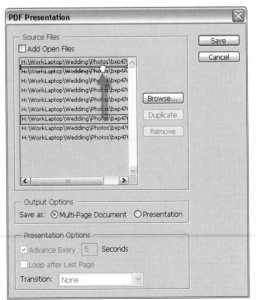

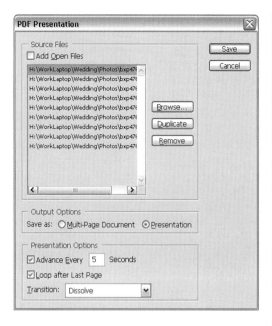

STEP TWO:

In the Output Options section, you can choose your regular Multi-Page Document PDF or you can select Presentation. Since the whole point of this is to present images to someone, let's choose Presentation here. Once you do this, the Presentation Options below will become enabled and you can choose how many seconds between each slide, whether or not to start over again after the presentation is done, and what type of transition you want between each slide. After you make these choices, click Save.

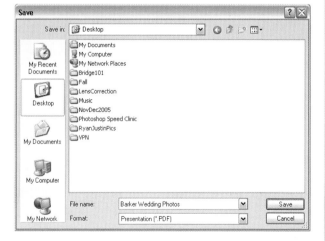

STEP THREE:

The next step is to pick where you want to save this PDF. Most of the time, I'll just save it to the Desktop and name the file based on the photo shoot.

TURBO BOOST

If you're paging through a PDF in Slide Show mode in Bridge and you decide you want to skip the rest of the PDF and move to the next image, just press Command-Right Arrow (PC: Control-Right Arrow).

STEP FOUR:

The last dialog you'll see is the Save Adobe PDF dialog. Here's where you make all of your choices about the PDF itself. Now, at first it may seem like there are a lot of choices here and, well, there are. Don't worry, though—there are only a few key ones that you'll need to worry about. First, you'll need to choose a quality setting from the Adobe PDF Preset pop-up menu. If you're emailing this presentation to someone, then it's usually best to choose Smallest File Size. However, if you want a high-quality PDF, suitable for printing, then choose High Quality Print. Also, if you're going to put this onto a webpage, then turn on the Optimize for Fast Web Preview checkbox in the Options section. Finally, I usually turn on the View PDF After Saving checkbox as well, so I can see the final result when I'm done.

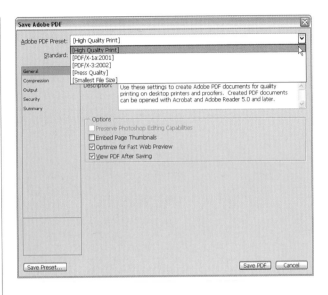

STEP FIVE:

The only other option that you'll really need to worry about if you want to get through this quickly is Security. Click on Security in the list on the left side of the dialog. On the right side, you'll see the options change. If you're posting this to a webpage and don't want anyone other than the person it's intended for to view it, then turn on the Require a Password to Open the Document checkbox in the Document Open Password section. Then, enter a password in the Document Open Password field. Don't forget to remember the password so you can give it to your client.

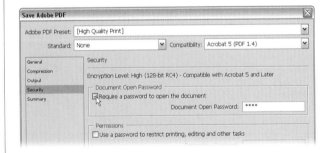

TURBO BOOST

Many people want to control the order in which the images show up in PDF Presentation. If you're selecting the images in Bridge be sure to move them into the order that you want them to display.

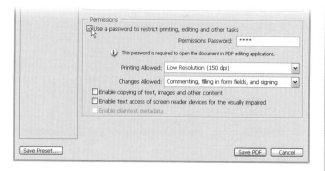

STEP SIX:
The next section is actually very useful. Let's say you created a high-quality PDF so your images look their best. However, you don't want people printing these images until they've paid for them. You can turn on the Use a Password to Restrict Printing, Editing, and Other Tasks checkbox in the Permissions section. Then create another password and enter it in the Permissions Password field. (Have a second password in mind for this option because you can't use the same one for both security settings.) Once you've set the security settings, just click the Save PDF button and Photoshop will create the PDF wherever you saved it. If you selected View PDF After Saving in Step Four, then the PDF should open, as well.

 Be sure to remember the Document Open and Permissions passwords that you create for the security settings. Not only will you and your client need them to open and work with the PDF presentation, but you will also be asked to confirm them when you are finished creating your presentation.

TURBO BOOST

If you're image processing a group of RAW files taken under the same lighting conditions, select Open First Image to Apply Settings, adjust the setting in the first image, and Image Processor will apply the same settings to all.

GETTING YOUR PORTFOLIO ON THE WEB (AND CUSTOMIZING IT!)

At Photoshop World Boston in September 2005, I taught a class called Getting Your Portfolio on the Web. It was all about getting photos on the Web and concentrated heavily on the Web Photo Gallery. I was amazed to see how many people knew the Web Photo Gallery was there but still had questions as to what really was going on. The first part of this tutorial involves creating the Web Photo Gallery. Luckily, there's not much to it since Photoshop does most of the hard work for you.

STEP ONE:

In Bridge, select the photos that you want to add to the Web Photo Gallery. Then choose Tools>Photoshop>Web Photo Gallery. This launches you into the Web Photo Gallery automation in Photoshop and opens the dialog that walks you through the process of creating the gallery.

STEP TWO:

The first choice in the Web Photo Gallery dialog is one of the most important and has actually been improved in CS2. The Styles setting affects how your Web gallery is going to look. In addition to HTML templates, Adobe has actually added Flash-based Web galleries in CS2. For this example, let's just choose Horizontal Neutral from the Styles pop-up menu. You can also add an email address so visitors to the gallery can contact you.

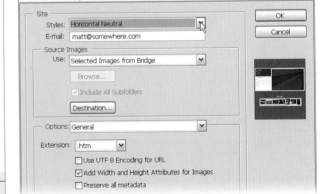

TURBO BOOST

Here's one a lot of people miss. When you're creating a Flash Web Photo Gallery, look on the right side of the dialog, below the preview, for instructions on how to add music to your Web gallery.

©MATT KLOSKOWSKI

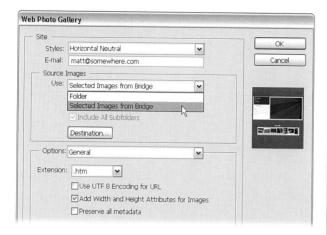

STEP THREE:

In the Source Images section, you can change the Use choice but since we launched from Bridge, we've already picked the images we want. Click the Destination button to tell Photoshop where you want to save your gallery. I usually just create a new folder on the Desktop to hold the webpage.

STEP FOUR:

In the Options section, you can do as much or as little as you want to change the gallery options. If you want to leave them alone, then go right ahead. For this example, though, choose Banner from the Options pop-up menu, enter a Site Name, and then enter your name as the Photographer (the Date field will automatically populate with the current date).

STEP FIVE:

That's it. Click OK to run the automation and build your Web gallery. Photoshop will do its thing for a moment. It will resize each selected photo to build a thumbnail and large image and then place them into the Web template. When it's done, you'll see the webpage launch in a browser. Keep in mind that the webpage is not live yet. You'll need to take the contents of the folder that you created and upload it to your website hosting company.

TURBO BOOST

Want a new or different Flash gallery? Don't waste time creating one. Adobe has another Flash gallery, along with instructions on how to install it, at www .adobe.com/support/downloads/detail .jsp?ftpID=2960.

©MATT KLOSKOWSKI

CUSTOMIZING THE WEB PHOTO GALLERY

Now that you've created the Web Photo Gallery, you may want to customize it. For example, a common question I get is how to add a custom logo in place of the default logo. Let's take a look at how to do that here.

STEP ONE:

Close your webpage and open the folder where you stored the Web Photo Gallery. Inside, you'll see a few files and a few folders. Open the images folder. On a Mac, make sure you have Show Preview Column turned on in Finder's View Options. In Windows, switch your folder view to thumbnails. If you look through the images in this folder, you'll see an image that looks just like the logo on the webpage (it's called "camicon02.gif"). This is the one that you'll need to replace.

TURBO BOOST

Want a little insider lingo tip? If you want to look cool in front of all your friends and family, then call a Web Photo Gallery "WPG" instead. That's just the hip way to refer to it and I know you want to be hip, right?

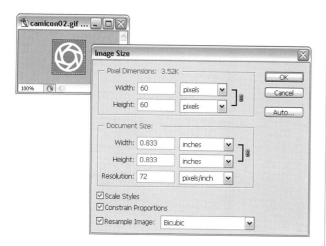

STEP TWO:

Open the camicon02.gif image in Photoshop. If you choose Image>Image Size you'll see the size of this image (60x60 pixels, in this case). This is the size of the logo that you'll need to create in order for it to fit in the webpage. Close the image and create a new 60x60-pixel file and add your logo to it.

STEP THREE:

Save your new logo as "camicon02.gif" and be sure to overwrite the existing one in the images folder. Now, view the index .html file again and you will see your new logo in place of the old one at the top.

TURBO BOOST

If you're an HTML-savvy person, you can edit the source files for all Web Photo Galleries in the Web Photo Gallery folder in Photoshop CS2's Presets folder. Just be sure to back up the originals in case you need to get them back.

USING A CONTACT SHEET TO FIND PHOTOS AFTER YOU BACK THEM UP TO CD

I often get questions from people asking how they can find their images once they've backed them up to CD or DVD. I don't blame them for asking. Especially with the growing popularity of shooting RAW and the large file sizes, you've got to start backing up photos. If you've got a bunch of disks laying around with all of your photos, how are you supposed to remember what is on them without placing each one into your CD drive and looking? Luckily, there's an easier way called a contact sheet.

Step One:

In Bridge, navigate to the CD containing the photos you've backed up or a folder containing any images that you want to create a contact sheet from. Select the images that you want to add to the contact sheet and choose Tools>Photoshop>Contact Sheet II. This will launch Photoshop if it's not open already and open the Contact Sheet II dialog.

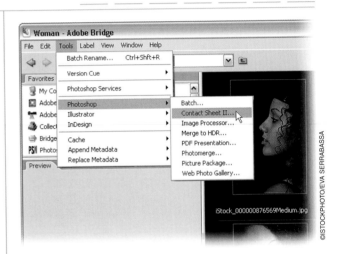

Step Two:

Since you began this from Bridge, the Use field should already be populated with Selected Images from Bridge. The rest of the options here will determine how your thumbnails will be displayed on the contact sheet. The first thing you'll need to do is decide how large you want this document. If you're creating a document for a CD jewel case, you should use 4.75x4.75". If you just want a regular sheet to preview your images, then you can leave the defaults of 8x10". Also, change the resolution setting to something lower, like 100 or 150 ppi.

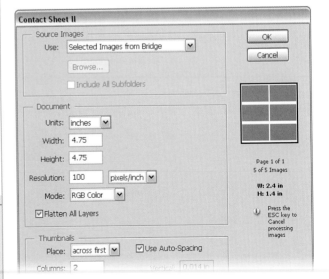

TURBO BOOST

Turn on the Flatten All Layers checkbox in the Contact Sheet II dialog to flatten all photo thumbnails and captions onto one layer. If you don't choose this option, you could wind up with a large, multilayered Photoshop file.

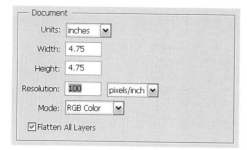

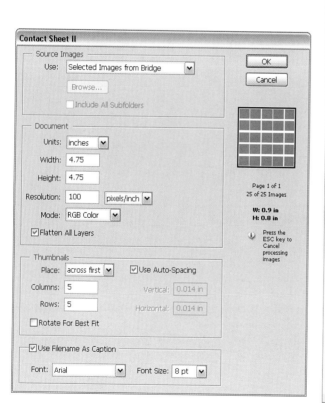

Setting a high resolution here is kind of pointless. Change it to a lower setting since these are small thumbnails anyway and you won't notice any image degradation. Plus, it makes the automation run faster.

STEP THREE:
The next section of the dialog, Thumbnails, tells Photoshop how you want your images placed in the contact sheet. There's even a small preview area on the right so you can see what the layout will look like. I know, they're just small gray boxes but hey, at least it's something, right? The first thing you'll want to do is decide how many images you want in each column and row. This is one of those situations where you have to strike a balance between showing a lot of images and making them large enough so you can actually see them. I've found that 6 columns and rows is the max I usually use here (if you can get away with 5 and 5, then go for it).

TURBO BOOST

In Step Three of this tutorial, make sure you choose a small font size so you can see the full name of your images on the contact sheet. Otherwise, larger file names may be cut off depending on the thumbnail size.

STEP FOUR:

Lastly, if you want to be able to figure out which image you're looking at, then make sure to turn on the Use Filename as Caption checkbox near the bottom of the dialog. Otherwise, you'll still need to look through all of the photos to find the right one. If you know the name, though, you can search for it and find it much quicker.

STEP FIVE:

You're ready to let Contact Sheet II do its thing. Click OK and it'll work its magic. In the end, you'll be left with a Photoshop file containing all of your images on one sheet. Just print it out and place it in your jewel case (if that's the size you created) and you can quickly find your images when you need them.

TURBO BOOST

When using the Web Photo Gallery, don't try to resize all of your images for the Web ahead of time. The WPG automation takes care of the resizing for you.

My wife, Diana, isn't much of a Photoshop user. She likes to fool around and fix photos every once in a while but she doesn't know all of the ins-and-outs of the program (that's why she has me, right?). Well, one day she wanted to create some prints of our kids to send to her family. She was trying to save paper and ink by resizing photos and fitting them onto a page manually. I wish you could have seen the look on her face when I showed her the Picture Package automation that did this for her in just a minute or two.

CREATING YOUR OWN PICTURE PACKAGES

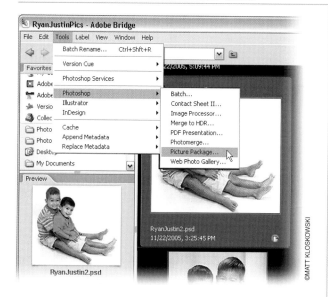

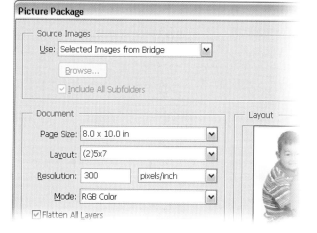

©MATT KLOSKOWSKI

PART ONE: CREATING A BASIC PICTURE PACKAGE

STEP ONE:

Let's start off in Bridge. By default, Picture Package will use the first image in the Bridge window so select the photo (or photos) that you want to use. Then choose Tools>Photoshop>Picture Package. You'll see the Picture Package dialog open in Photoshop. Similar to the other automations, you'll see the Source Images section at the top. Here you can decide to change the Use field from Selected Images from Bridge to another option, if you'd like.

TURBO BOOST

If you don't like the size of the images that the WPG produces, there's no need to try to resize them yourself. Just look in the Options section when creating the WPG and change either the Thumbnails or Large Images setting.

STEP TWO:

Next, in the Document section you can choose the overall document options. For this example, choose 8.0 x 10.0 in as the Page Size setting. For Layout, choose the second option in the pop-up menu, (1)5x7 (2)2.5x3.5 (4)2x2.5, to print on the same page. When you do this, you'll see the Layout section on the right side of the dialog change to reflect your choices. Set the resolution of the page, as well as the color mode. I've dropped the Resolution down to 200 and set the Mode to RGB Color, since I'm only printing to a desktop inkjet printer. Turn on the Flatten All Layers checkbox so that the images and any labels (text) will be flattened down to one layer in Photoshop.

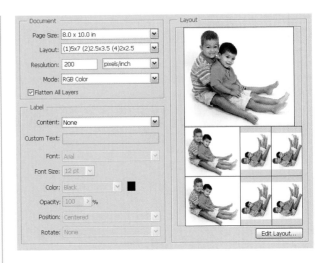

STEP THREE:

In the Label section, choose None for Content. What you choose here will be put on each photo. That's really it for this part. You can click OK now to create the picture package image, or you could be adventurous and read on—you'll see how you can customize the picture package so you can create your own.

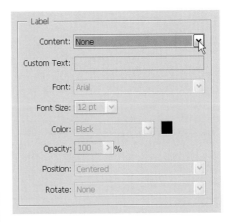

 Deselecting Flatten All Layers will cause all of the photos and any label text to appear on separate layers. You may think that this gives you more flexibility, but really it can just be a pain and it takes longer for the automation to run. Stick with Flatten All Layers for most cases.

TURBO BOOST

In Step Two of this tutorial, you can change the Picture Package layout by choosing a different option. However, you can also click on one of the photos in the Layout section to select a custom image to use instead of the default photo.

PART TWO: CUSTOMIZING PICTURE PACKAGES

Let's say you have a bunch of 4x6" picture frames lying around your house and you want to create prints to fit in them. Since none of the custom layouts meets these needs, it's time to take things into your own hands and create your own.

STEP FOUR:

Follow Steps One and Two in Part One to start creating a picture package. After you've changed the layout option, move your cursor over one of the photos in the Layout section. You'll see a tip telling you to Click to Select a Custom File. If you click on one of the photos, you'll see the Select an Image File (creative name, isn't it?) dialog appear. Here you can select another image in place of the one you clicked on, and just click Open to have it replaced.

Don't be fooled into thinking this option will change all of the photos in the layout. Clicking on a photo only changes the one that you selected. It leaves the others alone.

TURBO BOOST

When creating your own custom picture packages, it's best to start out with a template that is close to what you want to create. You can then easily add, delete, or change zones without having to create the entire template from scratch.

©MATT KLOSKOWSKI

STEP FIVE:

You can also edit the overall layout of the Picture Package. First, in the Picture Package dialog, select the (1)5x7 (2)3.5x5 Layout option to use as a starting point. Then click the Edit Layout button in the bottom-right corner of the dialog. You'll see the Picture Package Edit Layout dialog appear.

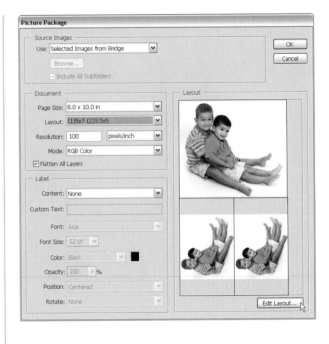

STEP SIX:

In the Layout section, give your layout a descriptive name. Here, you can enter any custom Page Size, Width, and Height settings, as well. Before you move on to the Image Zones section, turn on the Snap To checkbox in the Grid section at the bottom of the dialog and enter 0.5 in for the Size setting.

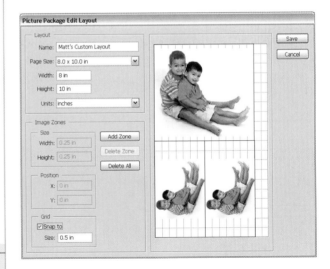

TURBO BOOST

Be sure to check out the first tutorial in Chapter 5 to learn how to create your own flexible custom picture package using Smart Objects.

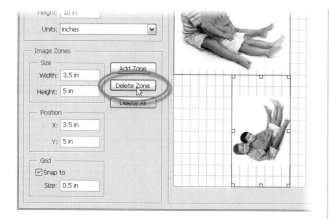

STEP SEVEN:

Next, delete the two bottom photos (the two 3.5x5" photos) by clicking on one of them and then clicking the Delete Zone button in the Image Zones section. Do the same for the other photo.

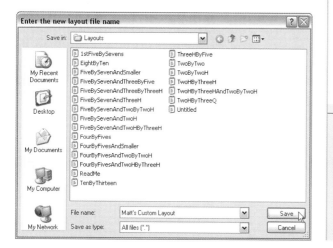

STEP EIGHT:

Click once on the top photo (the 5x7" photo) and in the Image Zones section change the Size Width to 6 in and the Height to 4 in. Then click the Add Zone button to create another 6x4" picture in this layout. Position the photos in the center of the layout by clicking-and-dragging them until they snap into place. When you're done, click Save and enter the new layout file name in the resulting dialog to save this new layout. Click Save and you'll be back in the original Picture Package dialog where you can finish off the automation by pressing OK.

TURBO BOOST

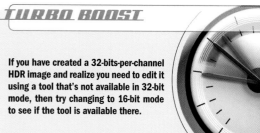

If you have created a 32-bits-per-channel HDR image and realize you need to edit it using a tool that's not available in 32-bit mode, then try changing to 16-bit mode to see if the tool is available there.

CREATING A KILLER PANORAMA

Believe it or not, a lot of people don't know that Photoshop can automatically stitch your photos together for you to create a panorama. If you continue reading this, then I'm guessing you fall into the "believe it" category and that's fine—you're why I've included this tutorial here. Honestly, when I show people where this feature is and that it's really called Photomerge instead of Create Panorama, they always say, "I saw that but I just never thought to use it for a panorama."

STEP ONE:
Open Bridge and select the photos you want to include in this pano. (By the way, the word pano is pro-speak for panorama. You know those pros, right? They just hate saying the full word.) Once you have the photos selected, choose Tools>Photoshop>Photomerge. The photos are then opened and assembled automatically. Photoshop will think for a moment as it tries to stitch the photos together. If you're lucky, the first dialog you see after this will be the Photomerge dialog and this will tell you that everything has gone okay—so far.

©MATT KLOSKOWSKI

TURBO BOOST

Another great speed tip to help your panorama photos out before you even get into Photoshop is to shoot the photos vertically, not horizontally, and overlap each one by approximately 15%.

 If you're unlucky and the composition can't be automatically assembled, a warning appears onscreen letting you know. Have no fear, though—you can always create the composition manually in the Photomerge dialog using the Lightbox at the top of the dialog. This is where you can make some specific decisions on how Photoshop treats the merged photos.

STEP TWO:

The first area to check out on the right side of the Photomerge dialog is the Settings section. Most of the time, you'll wind up leaving this set to Normal. Perspective is used when you're shooting a pano that is 180 or 360° around. Now, if you do shoot one of those panos and click on the Perspective radio button, you'll see another option become available called Cylindrical Mapping in the Composition Settings section. Turn on this checkbox to reduce the bowed distortion that can appear when shooting these types of panos.

TURBO BOOST

Even though Photoshop can work wonders on your panoramas, it's best to give them a good start. If you really want to speed up the panorama stitching process, then make sure you shoot your photos on a tripod.

STEP THREE:

Finally, lighting conditions can cause various issues in your stitched photos. Sometimes the auto exposure settings on your camera can cause seams to become visible between photos. Turning on the Advanced Blending checkbox, in the Composition Settings section, can sometimes help alleviate these seams. Be sure to click the Preview button to see if it makes things better or worse. One more thing...let's say you want to keep each image in the pano separate from each other so you can edit them individually in Photoshop. Just turn on the Keep as Layers checkbox at the bottom of the dialog. You'll want to select this option if you think you'll need to do some color or lighting correction on individual photos.

You can't select Keep as Layers and Advanced Blending at the same time. You'll need to make a decision as to which one you'd rather use.

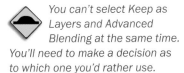

When you're creating a panorama using Photomerge, you can save the stitch options and progress by pressing the Save Composition As button in the top-right corner.

STEP FOUR:

When you're done, just click OK and Photoshop will process the photos and build your panorama. It may take a few minutes depending on the number and size of your photos. When it's done you'll see the panorama open in Photoshop.

STEP FIVE:

The last thing you may need to do to finish this off is to straighten and crop the pano. Straightening photos in Photoshop CS2 (which is really easy, by the way) is covered in Chapter 9 on page 186. As for cropping, you'll most likely see some transparent areas on the top or bottom of the image. Just select the Crop tool (C) and crop the image so those areas are gone.

TURBO BOOST

When creating a pano, 16-bits-per-channel images and 32-bits-per-channel images are converted to 8-bits-per-channel images.

CONVERTING MULTIPLE IMAGES FROM ONE FILE TYPE TO ANOTHER

I can't even begin to count the number of times people have asked me how to convert an entire folder of RAW files into PSD, TIFF, or JPEG files. I used to cringe when I got the question, though, because it involved creating an action and batch processing. It wasn't difficult to do but it just wasn't the quick one-minute answer they wanted. However, in Photoshop CS2, I now have my quick one-minute answer. Heck, it's really a 10-second answer—it's called Image Processor and it rocks!

STEP ONE:

Let's say you're a photographer and just got back from a photo shoot. It could be a professional shoot or just a day out with the kids. Either way, it's likely you've got a lot of images that need processing. If you shot in RAW, you'll have to convert those photos to an easier format for sharing and printing. Also, it's likely you'll need to resize your photos, as well, so you can email them to family or friends or put them on a website. The first thing to do is go find the photos in Bridge that you need to process. In this example, I'm going to use RAW images but it could just as easily be JPEG or TIFF. Choose Tools>Photoshop>Image Processor and the Image Processor dialog will appear.

STEP TWO:

The nice folks at Adobe numbered the Image Processor dialog with four sections so it makes it easy to work with. In the first section, choose a folder of the images you want to process. Since we launched this through Bridge, your images should already be selected and it'll tell you how many will be processed. You can also choose to work with open images if you have some open in Photoshop already.

TURBO BOOST

Before you process your images, click Save to save the current settings in the dialog. The next time you need to process files using this group of settings, click Load and navigate to your saved Image Processor settings.

Image Processor

1. Select the images to process
   Process files from Bridge only (8)
   ☐ Open first image to apply settings

2. Select location to save processed images
   ⦿ Save in Same Location
   ○ [Select Folder...] No folder has been select

○ [Select Folder...] No folder has been selected

3. **File Type**

☑ Save as JPEG   ☑ Resize to Fit
Quality: 10   W: 640 px
☑ Convert Profile to sRGB   H: 480 px

☐ Save as PSD   ☐ Resize to Fit
  ☑ Maximize Compatibility   W: [ ] px
                        H: [ ] px

☑ Save as TIFF   ☐ Resize to Fit
  ☐ LZW Compression   W: [ ] px
                        H: [ ] px

4. Preferences

STEP THREE:

In the second section, choose a destination. You can choose to save your images in the same location as the originals or you can pick a different location. I usually leave this set to Save in Same Location.

STEP FOUR:

In the third section, you'll need to pick what file type you want to save the images as. Your choices are JPEG, PSD, and TIFF. You can pick any one, a combination, or all three of the file types if you choose. Photoshop will create an individual folder for each file type and a copy of your photo for each option you select. You'll also notice there are options for resizing the images, as well. Let's go ahead and select JPEG with a quality setting of 10. Turn on the Resize to Fit checkbox and enter 640 for width and 480 for height. Now, this doesn't resize each image to fit into 640x480, though. What it does is set a maximum size constraint so photos will be a maximum of 640 pixels wide and 480 pixels high. But, it doesn't change the aspect ratio, which is important to know. Finally, if you're sending files to a printer that may require them to be in the sRGB color profile, then turn on the Convert Profile to sRGB checkbox. While we're here, I'm also going to select Save as TIFF and leave these photos at their original size.

TURBO BOOST

The Copyright Info setting in the Image Processor dialog includes any text you enter in the IPTC copyright metadata for the file. Text you include here overwrites the copyright metadata in the original file, so make sure that is really what you want to do.

STEP FIVE:

Finally, in the fourth section, you have the option of running an action on each of the images that will be processed. This is convenient if, say, you have an action that creates a watermark on your photos automatically or even a sharpening action. You can run that action on all of these photos during this process. The last thing to choose is whether you want to add any copyright info, as well as whether to include the ICC profile. I suggest you do both here as these options may save you time down the road.

STEP SIX:

That's all there is to it. Once you've set all of the options, just click Run and watch Photoshop do its thing. Depending on how many images you're processing this could take anywhere from a few seconds to a few (or more) minutes. However, it's well worth the wait. In the end, you'll see two new folders containing your new images.

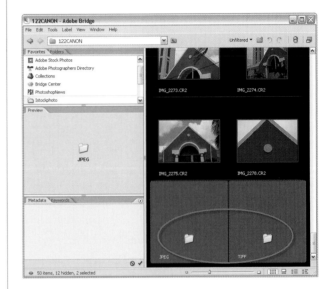

Keep in mind that digital cameras produce some very large RAW files. If you select a folder with 100 RAW images in it, be prepared to wait 5 or 10 minutes for Image Processor to run. However, it's still faster than doing it yourself.

TURBO BOOST

When processing Camera Raw files with Image Processor, the settings you apply with the Image Processor are temporary and used only with the Image Processor. The image's current Camera Raw settings are used to process the image, unless you change them in the Image Processor.

A few years ago my wife went on a digital-photo printing spree. All of a sudden, she had to have photos of our sons printed and in albums and it had to be done *now*. (I, naturally, didn't resist.) We had one problem, though. Whenever she downloaded the photos from the camera onto the computer, they were too big and needed a few adjustments (sharpening, lightening, etc.). To make things worse, she had no idea how to use Photoshop. So I came up with a great solution. I created a droplet that did everything for her. She didn't even have to open Photoshop to use it.

RUNNING ACTIONS OUTSIDE OF PHOTOSHOP

WHAT IS A DROPLET?

A droplet is a little application that sits outside of Photoshop and works very much like the Batch command does (see Chapter 4 for everything you ever wanted to know about batch processing). You need Photoshop to create a droplet, but you don't need to know anything about using Photoshop to run a droplet, so it's great for a photographer's assistant who doesn't want to learn Photoshop but can still help out. Even better, if you read Chapter 4 you'll know everything there is to learn about batch processing and creating a droplet is almost identical. In fact, the dialogs look nearly the same, so there's not much new to learn here.

TURBO BOOST

You can create a droplet inside of Image-Ready just like you can in Photoshop. In ImageReady, just choose **Create Droplet** from the Actions palette's flyout menu to turn your action into a droplet.

STEP ONE:

Open Photoshop and go to the File menu. Choose Automate>Create Droplet and you'll see the Create Droplet dialog open. The first thing you'll need to do here is pick where you want to save this droplet. Note that you're not picking where you want to save the images that the droplet will produce, just where you want to save the droplet icon itself. I usually set this to the Desktop.

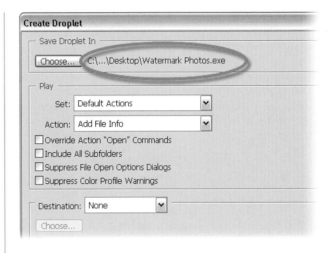

STEP TWO:

Just like in the Batch dialog, choose an action to run here. In this example, I'm going to use the same action that was used in the Batch Processing chapter. In fact, the rest of the settings are the same as in the Batch dialog, so go ahead and set them now. Feel free to refer back to Chapter 4 if you need a refresher on what they do.

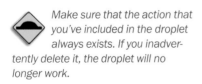 *Make sure that the action that you've included in the droplet always exists. If you inadvertently delete it, the droplet will no longer work.*

If you create a Photoshop droplet in Windows and move it to Mac OS, you must drag the droplet icon onto the Photoshop icon first. Photoshop will then update the droplet for use in Mac OS.

STEP THREE:
Press OK when you're done to create the droplet. Nothing visible will really happen here and you haven't actually executed any action yet. You will however see a new icon on the Desktop with the name you gave it in Step One.

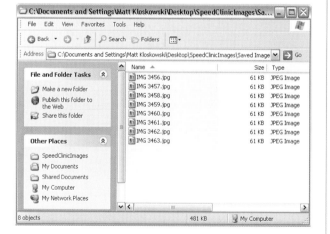

STEP FOUR:
To use the droplet, just drag any images (or even a folder of images) onto the droplet icon on your Desktop. If Photoshop isn't already open it will launch and start executing a batch process using the action you specified in the Create Droplet dialog. It will then put the resulting images in whatever destination folder you specified when creating the droplet.

When you create a droplet on the Mac, add the EXE extension to it to make the droplet compatible with both Windows and Mac OS if you plan on sharing it.

CREATING A HIGH DYNAMIC RANGE (HDR) IMAGE

I have to say that when I was at Photoshop World Boston in September 2005, I was surprised at how many people asked about the new Merge to HDR feature. I think what surprised me the most is the fact that so many people were interested in it even though the photos contain a dynamic range that exceeds what most printers, displays, and humans can interpret. Nonetheless, it is a speed-related feature and I think it's at least useful to know how to use it.

STEP ONE:

First, you'll need to shoot several versions (actually two or more) of your photograph with different exposures. See your camera's instruction guide to find out how to do this. The nice thing about using this new feature in Photoshop CS2 is that it's not limited to only those professional SLR cameras. Most of the basic point-and-shoot cameras also have settings for changing exposure.

One note of caution before you start, though. Many people have tried to fake multiple exposures inside of Photoshop. They then try to run those images through Merge to HDR and it just won't work. Sorry to be the bearer of bad news, but I'm just trying to save you some time.

TURBO BOOST

As cool as HDR may sound, there aren't many monitors that can display these types of photos. Because of that, my speed tip here is to not spend too much time creating them because you really won't be able to show them off.

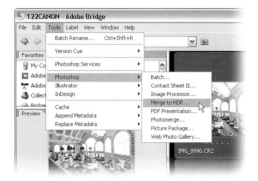

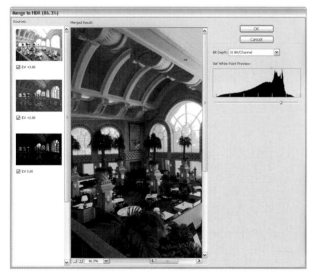

STEP TWO:

Next, select the photos in Bridge and choose Tools>Photoshop>Merge to HDR. Photoshop will think for a moment (or a few moments, depending on the size of the photos and your computer's speed) and then display the Merge to HDR dialog.

STEP THREE:

Here's where you can make a few adjustments based on your desired image output. First, you can click the checkbox under each image to preview what your final image will look like. All you really need to use Merge to HDR is two photos. This option gives you a good way to figure out if your final image will look better or worse if you don't include more images.

TURBO BOOST

Try not to use your camera's auto-bracket feature to create HDR images. The exposure changes are usually too small and the automation may not even run.

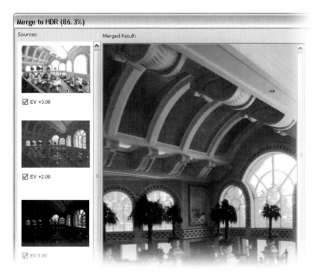

STEP FOUR:

On the right side of the dialog, from the Bit Depth pop-up menu, you can choose what bit depth setting you'd like to use. For the best quality possible, and to create a true HDR image, choose 32 Bit/Channel. It's possible to use the Merge to HDR command to save the merged image as an 8- or 16-bits-per-channel image. However, only a 32-bits-per-channel image can store all the HDR image data; 8- and 16-bits-per-channel images will begin to lose some of the dynamic range that you'd use Merge to HDR for in the first place.

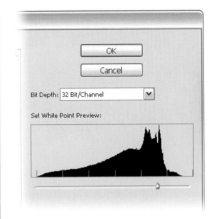

 32-bit images have a very limited number of tools and functions that can be applied to them. It's good to be aware of this, as when you're back in Photoshop you'll likely see most filters and adjustments grayed out and you won't be able to use them.

STEP FIVE:

Next, you can adjust the slider under Set White Point Preview to set the white point. Honestly, the default setting here usually works best, but feel free to experiment. Then, click OK and Photoshop will do the merging for you. Don't worry, your originals won't be harmed. Photoshop will merge the images and open a brand new image in a new document.

TURBO BOOST

You can use the Merge to HDR command to save the merged image as an 8- or 16-bits-per-channel image. However, only a 32-bits-per-channel image can store all the HDR image data, so there's really no point in using a smaller bit depth.

TURBO BOOST

You can also use Merge to HDR on scanned photos. The only trick is that Photoshop will pop open a dialog asking you for the exposure settings used when you took the photo, so make sure you know them ahead of time.

CHAPTER 8

PHOTOSHOP FOR GEEKS—THE POWER OF SCRIPTING

SCRIPTING ISN'T JUST FOR CODING GEEKS ANYMORE

I'm introducing this chapter by making a disclaimer. Now, I know it's never good to start a chapter that way, is it? But I promise it's nothing bad—I just want to set the stage for what's to come in the following pages. Scripting in Photoshop can be considered an advanced task. However, I don't want to scare you away. If you set your mind to learning how to write scripts then you can indeed learn, but it will take some work. This chapter is really only meant to be an introduction and to show you what can be accomplished. It would take an entire book or two to really get in-depth with this subject, so I encourage you to review the last part of Chapter 11, where I point you to some great resources.

WORKING WITH SCRIPTS IN PHOTOSHOP

Many people are surprised when I tell them my background. I actually graduated from college with a computer programming degree and worked as a software developer for nearly eight years. It was during that time that I developed my passion for the creative side of working on the computer and using Photoshop, but I still always have a part of me that likes to work with code, too. That's why I'm excited to see how popular scripting is getting in Photoshop.

STEP ONE:

By default, Photoshop CS2 includes scripts you can use on your images. Just open Photoshop and choose File>Scripts to see a list of what scripts are included with CS2.

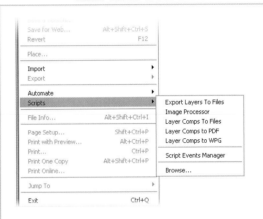

STEP TWO:

In this example, let's try out the Image Processor script by choosing File>Scripts> Image Processor. This is a new script included in Photoshop CS2 and is almost worth the price of the upgrade alone. As you can see, the dialog looks very similar to the other dialogs that you'll see in Photoshop. The key difference is that this one was created inside a script that can be edited (unlike the Automations that appear under the File>Automate menu).

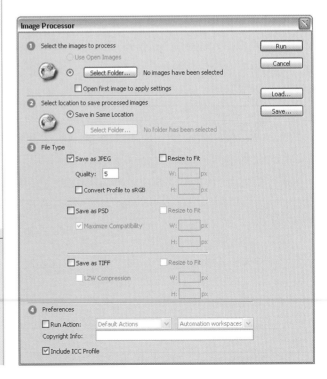

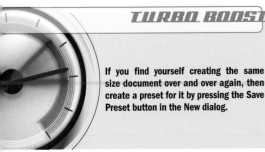

TURBO BOOST

If you find yourself creating the same size document over and over again, then create a preset for it by pressing the Save Preset button in the New dialog.

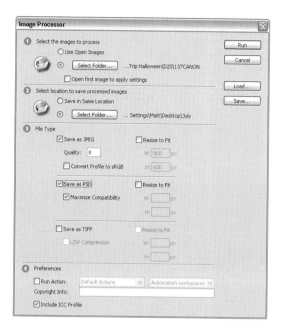

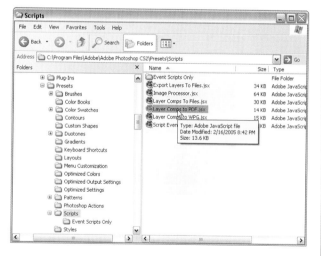

STEP THREE:

Enter all the necessary information for this script as described in Chapter 7 on page 140 and click OK to run the script. See...there's nothing really different about scripts and the way they work.

STEP FOUR:

You can also navigate to any scripts on your file system and run them directly without going through Photoshop. Just go to your Photoshop CS2 Presets folder and look inside the Scripts folder. (On a Mac, go to Hard Drive:Applications:Adobe Photoshop CS2:Presets:Scripts. On a PC, go to C:\Program Files\Adobe\Adobe Photoshop CS2\Presets\Scripts.)

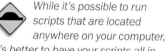

While it's possible to run scripts that are located anywhere on your computer, it's better to have your scripts all in one place. Overall, it'll make it a lot easier and faster to manage them. See Installing a New Script on the next page to find out where to store your scripts.

TURBO BOOST

A single script can perform actions that involve multiple applications. For example, you could target both Photoshop CS2 and another Adobe Creative Suite 2 application in the same script.

INSTALLING A NEW SCRIPT: ADDING FILE NAMES TO PDF PRESENTATION

One day, my boss, Scott Kelby, called me into his office and said that he's gotten a lot of questions about why PDF Presentation doesn't include file names on the images. The problem is that it leaves your client wondering which photos they like best, as they have no way to tell you other than by numeric order (which can be difficult and unreliable). We talked about how cool it would be to create a script to do it, and that is exactly what I did after that meeting.

STEP ONE:
Download the script I created that adds file names to all of the images you put into a PDF presentation from www.scottkelbybooks.com/speedclinic. Unzip the file and place the script somewhere on your computer where you can easily find it (the Desktop is always a good place).

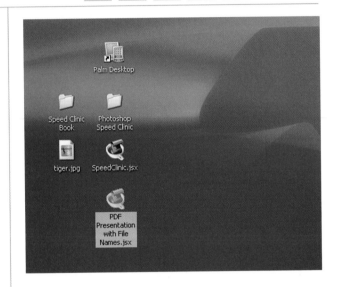

STEP TWO:
Navigate to your Photoshop CS2 Presets folder and look for the Scripts folder within it. On the Mac, go to Hard Drive: Applications:Adobe Photoshop CS2:Presets:Scripts. On a PC, go to C:\Program Files\Adobe\Adobe Photoshop CS2\Presets\Scripts. Place the script that you downloaded in Step One into this folder.

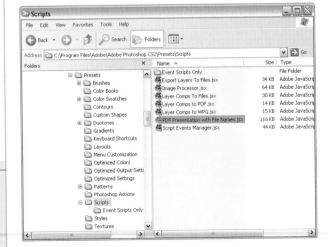

TURBO BOOST

Moving a layer mask from one layer to another layer just got easier with Photoshop CS2. Try just clicking-and-dragging the layer mask to whatever layer you'd like in the Layers palette.

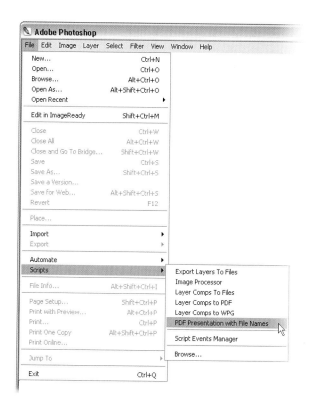

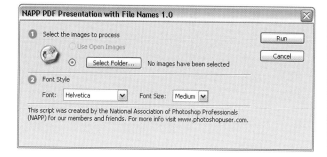

Scripting in Photoshop is not new to CS2. That's why you need to be careful when you install a script. Be sure that it is meant for the version of Photoshop that you're using. You don't want to spend a bunch of time installing a script that won't run in your version of Photoshop. This script happens to be for Photoshop CS2 only.

STEP THREE:

Before Photoshop will recognize this script and show it under the File>Scripts menu, you'll need to restart Photoshop. So, if you have Photoshop running, shut it down and restart it. If you don't have it running, then go ahead and fire up Photoshop CS2 now. When you do, choose File>Scripts and you should now see PDF Presentation with File Names. The script is installed and ready to use.

Be careful when installing a script because all of the other CS2 applications, including Bridge, can be scripted, as well. You'll want to make sure you're installing a script that is meant for Photoshop and not for Bridge or one of the other applications.

TURBO BOOST

Quickly put multiple layers into a Group (formerly a Layer Set) by selecting them in the Layers palette and pressing Command-G (PC: Control-G).

CREATING, EDITING, AND TESTING SCRIPTS (THE EXTEND-SCRIPT TOOLKIT)

When I first started writing scripts for Photoshop, I used a plain old text editor. It worked fine, but it was a somewhat laborious task to write the scripts and then switch over to Photoshop to test them. Plus, troubleshooting the scripts was a difficult process, as well. Then I discovered the ExtendScript Toolkit in Photoshop CS2. Thankfully, it's a script editor that was created specifically for editing scripts in Photoshop and it really helps speed things up.

STEP ONE:
First, you'll need to find the ExtendScript Toolkit. You may have even seen it before but not known it. On the Mac, go to Hard Drive:Applications:Utilities:Adobe Utilities: ExtendScript Toolkit. In Windows, you'll find it on your Start Menu, under All Programs>Adobe>ExtendScript Toolkit.

STEP TWO:
Open the Toolkit editor. You'll see a window with Photoshop-like palettes on the left and a text editor on the right.

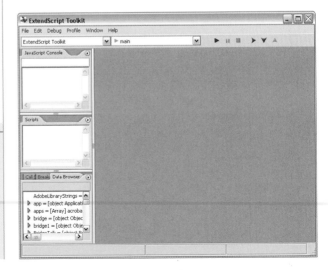

TURBO BOOST

If you're running or testing a script in the ExtendScript Toolkit and nothing seems to be happening, try clicking the Stop button to forcefully stop the script.

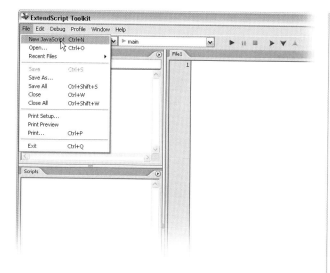

STEP THREE:

Choose File>New JavaScript. This will create a blank file with an area on the right ready for you to type.

You can write Photoshop scripts using JavaScript, VBScript (for Windows), or Applescript (for Mac OS). However, JavaScript is the only cross-platform scripting language, meaning it performs identically in both Windows and Mac OS. Keep this in mind, as you'll save yourself a lot of time by writing most of your scripts in Java-Script (as I have done throughout this tutorial), so everyone can use them.

STEP FOUR:

Type the text shown here into the text editor. This code creates a new dialog in Photoshop. I'd like to draw your attention to something, though. Look at Line 9. See how it contains the string dlg.txtName? This creates a text box in the new dialog for us to enter text. Behind the scenes, Photoshop is referring to this text box by its name, which is txtName. (*Note:* You can download this script at www.scottkelbybooks.com/speedclinic, in case you don't want to type in everything in Steps Four through Seven.)

```
1  var builder = createDialog();
2
3  builder.show();
4
5  function createDialog() {
6
7      var dlg = new Window('dialog', 'Gallery Print Script');
8      dlg.frameLocation = [100, 100];
9      dlg.txtName = dlg.add('edittext', undefined, 'Sample Text');
10     dlg.txtName.preferredSize = [200,20];
11     dlg.btnRun = dlg.add('button', undefined, 'Run');
12     return dlg;
13
14 }
15
```

TURBO BOOST

You can save JavaScript files with a JS or JSX extension on the end of them. If you use the JSX extension, the files will automatically open in the Extend-Script Toolkit.

STEP FIVE:

Now you'll need to test the script, which luckily is very easy when you're using the ExtendScript Toolkit. First, select Adobe Photoshop CS2 from the first pop-up menu on the top left. Next, click the Run button. Photoshop CS2 will be launched, if it isn't already. Then the window will switch over to Photoshop and your script will run behind the scenes.

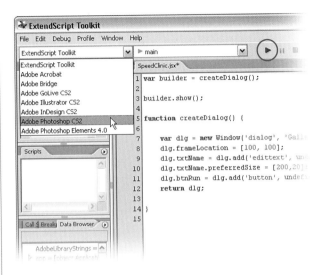

At this point, all we've done is create a dialog with a text box and a button. It should look like the dialog shown here.

STEP SIX:

This dialog won't actually do anything yet, though. To make it actually do something, type in the code shown here between your original Line 1 and your original Line 3 (which becomes Line 20, as you can see here).

TURBO BOOST

Check out the JavaScript Reference Guide in Adobe Photoshop CS2's Scripting Guide folder on your hard drive. It is the fastest way to get up to speed with scripting in Photoshop as well as the ExtendScript Toolkit.

```
1  var builder = createDialog();
2
3  builder.btnRun.onClick = function () {
4      var textColor = new SolidColor;
5      textColor.rgb.red = 0;
6      textColor.rgb.green = 0;
7      textColor.rgb.blue = 0;
8
9      var docRef = app.activeDocument;
10     var newTextLayer = docRef.artLayers.add();
11     newTextLayer.kind = LayerKind.TEXT;
12     newTextLayer.textItem.contents = builder.txtName.text;
13     newTextLayer.textItem.size = 24;
14     newTextLayer.textItem.color = textColor;
15
16     doAction("Gallery Print", "Speed Clinic.atn");
17     builder.close();
18 }
19
20 builder.show();
21
22 function createDialog() {
23
24     var dlg = new Window('dialog', 'Gallery Print Script');
25     dlg.frameLocation = [100, 100];
26     dlg.txtName = dlg.add('edittext', undefined, 'Sample Text');
27     dlg.txtName.preferredSize = [200,20];
28     dlg.btnRun = dlg.add('button', undefined, 'Run');
29     return dlg;
30
31 }
```

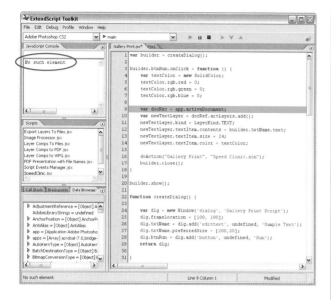

Be on the lookout for errors, as they can really slow you up if you don't know what to look for. You'll know pretty quickly because your computer should beep at you and you'll see a red line at the place of the error. ExtendScript Toolkit will even tell you what the error is in the JavaScript Console at the top left.

STEP SEVEN:

Now the script is done. However, before you run it take a look at Line 16. Notice it refers to an action called Gallery Print. You can actually call actions from scripts to really enhance the power you have to automate things in Photoshop. In order to use this script, be sure to download the Gallery Print action (Speed Clinic.atn) from www.scottkelbybooks.com/speed-clinic and load it into your Actions palette. If not, the script will not work. To load it into your Actions palette, first download the file into your Photoshop Actions folder, which is in Adobe Photoshop CS2's Presets folder. Then, from the Actions palette's flyout menu, choose Load Actions. In the resulting dialog, select Speed Clinic .atn and click Load. It should now appear at the bottom of your palette.

TURBO BOOST

Before you run a script using the Extend-Script Toolkit, you can check your code by choosing Edit>Check Syntax or press Command-Shift-K (PC: F7).

STEP EIGHT:

After you're done testing the script, you can name it "SpeedClinic" and save it into Photoshop CS2's Scripts folder, which is in the Presets folder. Then restart Photoshop, and it'll show up in the Scripts menu.

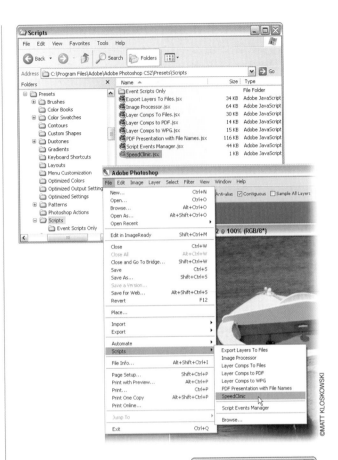

STEP NINE:

Open a photo in Photoshop. Choose File>Scripts>SpeedClinic and type in your name or a name for the photo in the text box. Press the Run button, and watch Photoshop work its magic by adding the text you entered and creating a gallery print from your photo. You'd never be able to use dynamic text in an action like this. An action would always add the same exact text. With a script, you can choose the text each time you run it.

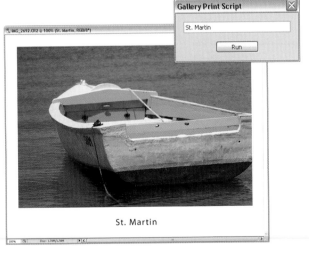

St. Martin

TURBO BOOST

When using the ExtendScript Toolkit, you can press Command-K (PC: Control-K) to get the Preferences dialog. Choose Font Options from the top pop-up menu to make the font size larger or smaller.

I recently wrote a feature article for *Photoshop User* magazine (Jan/Feb 2006) on the Script Events Manager. In doing so, I really realized the power that this new CS2 feature holds. Imagine that every time you created a new image in Photoshop, you could automatically have your copyright information attached to it. That would be a great insurance policy in case you ever forgot to add it later, wouldn't it? You can do just that with the Script Events Manager.

SETTING SCRIPTS AND ACTIONS TO RUN AUTOMATICALLY

STEP ONE:

Create a new blank file or open any image to start with. Honestly, it doesn't really matter how you start as long as you have a document open. I just figured I'd take any chance to show a photo of my lovely wife, Diana. After that, open the Actions palette and click the Create New Action icon to create a new action called Add Copyright Info. Click Record to start recording.

STEP TWO:

Choose File>File Info. Add any copyright information that you want associated with every new image you create in Photoshop. Click OK when you're done to save the file info. Then, click the Stop Recording icon to end the action.

TURBO BOOST

When using the Script Events Manager, you can disable and remove individual script events by selecting the event from the list and pressing the Remove button.

STEP THREE:

Now that the action is recorded, you'll have to create a script event that runs it after you create a new document. Choose File>Scripts>Script Events Manager. Turn on the Enable Events to Run Scripts/Actions checkbox.

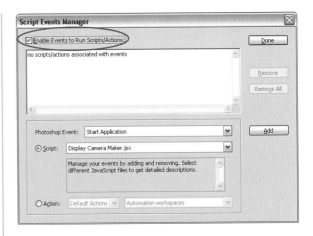

STEP FOUR:

For Photoshop Event, choose New Document from the pop-up menu. Click the Action radio button at the bottom of the dialog, and choose the Add Copyright Info action you just created from the list on the right. Click the Add button and close the dialog by clicking Done.

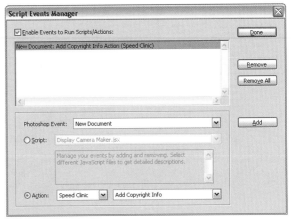

STEP FIVE:

Create a new document again. You probably won't see anything happen—because it happens so fast—but the Add Copyright Info action runs as soon as you click OK to create the new document. If you choose File>File Info, you will indeed see the copyright information you added in Step Two. As you can see, Photoshop did this automatically and will continue to do it each time you create a new document.

TURBO BOOST

In the Script Events Manager, you can disable script events but still keep them in the list by turning off the Enable Events to Run Scripts/Actions checkbox. They'll still be in the list but they won't run anymore.

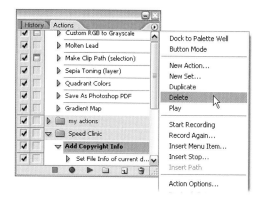

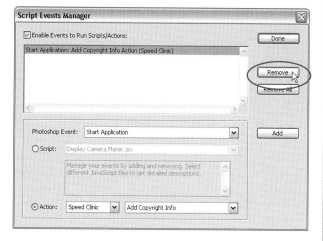

Keep in mind that this script event is tied to the action you created earlier. If you delete or change this action, then you're changing the action that the script event uses, too.

STEP SIX:
If you ever want to remove a script event, then continue reading. Choose File>Scripts>Script Events Manager. Click once on the script event in the list and click the Remove button. Click Done and the script event will no longer run every time you create a new document.

TURBO BOOST

In the Script Events Manager dialog, choose Add an Event from the Photoshop Event pop-up menu. Then look in Appendix A of the JavaScript Reference Guide (in Photoshop CS2's Scripting Guide folder) for ideas on which events you can add.

LETTING PHOTO-SHOP WRITE SCRIPTS FOR YOU (INSTALLING SCRIPT LISTENER)

One evening while watching some very useless television show, I was looking through some of the scripting guide files that come with Photoshop CS2 (yep, that's what I do at night). I stumbled across one of the best-kept secrets of writing scripts for Photoshop—Script Listener. You see, any tool that makes Photoshop do more of the work for me gets my vote, and that is exactly what the Script Listener does.

STEP ONE:

Locate the ScriptListener plug-in file. On a Mac, go to Hard Drive:Applications:Adobe Photoshop CS2:Scripting Guide:Utilities, and select the ScriptingListener.plugin file. On a PC, go to C:\Program Files\Adobe\Adobe Photoshop CS2\Scripting Guide\Utilities, and select the ScriptListener.8li file. Then choose Edit>Copy.

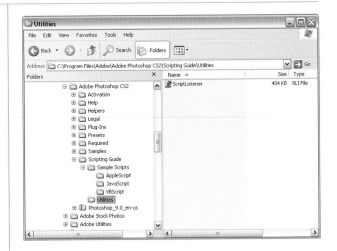

STEP TWO:

In the Adobe Photoshop CS2 folder, navigate to the Plug-Ins folder and in the Adobe Photoshop Only folder, select Automate. Choose Edit>Paste to paste the copy of the ScriptingListener.plugin or ScriptListener.8li file into the Automate folder.

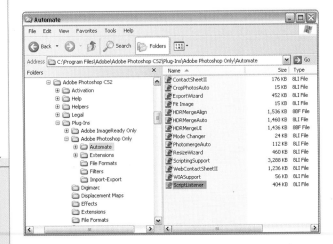

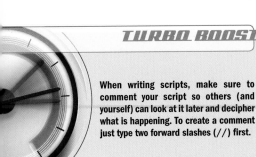

TURBO BOOST

When writing scripts, make sure to comment your script so others (and yourself) can look at it later and decipher what is happening. To create a comment just type two forward slashes (//) first.

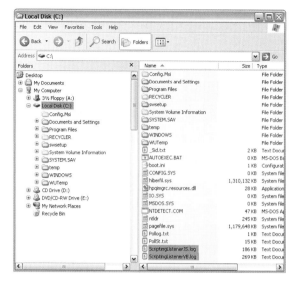

STEP THREE:

Now you need to open Photoshop CS2. If it's already open and you never closed it, go ahead and close it and then start it up again. The Script Listener will now create a log file of everything that you do in Photoshop. This file contains the JavaScript code that represents all of your commands and actions in Photoshop. (In Windows, a VBScript log file will also be created.) In Mac OS, Script Listener creates the file on your Desktop. In Windows, Script Listener places the files on your C:\ drive.

STEP FOUR:

To verify this is working, press Command-N (PC: Control-N) to create a new document. Enter 800 pixels for the width and 600 pixels for the height. Select the Type tool (T) and create some text that reads "Hello World." Don't worry about what font size or style you use at this point.

STEP FIVE:

Find the JavaScript log file and open it using a text editor. I have to warn you, though—this is not for those with weak hearts or those who frighten easily. This log file is really scary looking, but you should be able to see some familiar text in it (highlighted in the screen capture here). Look for the size of the new document that you created in Step Four. Also, you can see the text that you created, as well. Without getting too technical, these are the commands getting sent to Photoshop in the background; everything you do can be represented in this type of language.

TURBO BOOST

Adobe Bridge can run scripts, too. Be sure that if you install a third-party script you know whether it's intended for Photoshop or Bridge.

USING THE SCRIPT LISTENER

In this example, we're going to modify the script we created in the tutorial on page 156. However, we're going to do it with the Script Listener. Why, you ask? Because I need to fill a few more pages in the book. Just kidding, I'm probably already over my page count, but I do want to demonstrate what you can do with this plug-in. We're actually going to use it to add a drop shadow to a type layer because adding a layer style via script is really not as easy as you'd think. So instead, we'll let Photoshop write the code for us.

STEP ONE:
Open any photo in Photoshop. Create a new type layer with your name (or anything, for that matter) on it.

STEP TWO:
Click once on the type layer in the Layers palette to make it active. Delete the Script Listener JavaScript log file on your computer. Don't worry, you're not deleting the plug-in file that you added in the Installing Script Listener tutorial. The actual JavaScript log file will always automatically be recreated if you delete it. Also, make sure you only delete this file when you're absolutely ready to have Script Listener record your actions. Remember how ugly the code looked? You don't want to have to sift through all that to find your specific commands.

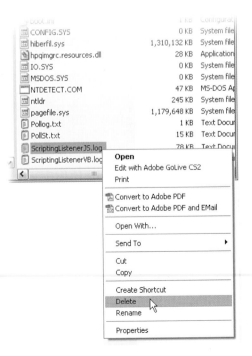

TURBO BOOST

You can manage Bridge-specific scripts in Bridge by choosing Edit>Script Manager.

©MATT KLOSKOWSKI

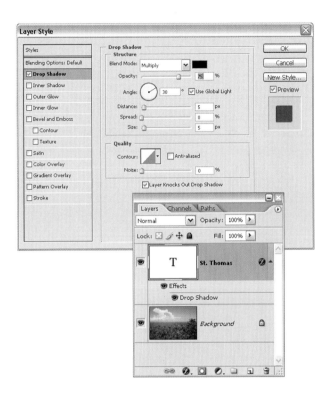

STEP THREE:

Since you just deleted the log file, whatever you do from this point will be recorded in a new JavaScript log file by Script Listener. Click on the Add a Layer Style icon at the bottom of the Layers palette and choose Drop Shadow from the pop-up menu. You can adjust the settings here or just use the defaults for this example. Click OK and don't do anything else. I repeat...don't do anything else in Photoshop, yet.

STEP FOUR:

Find the JavaScript log file and open it in any text editor. First, look at the ugly code that it generates and be thankful that you don't have to type that yourself. Then press Command-A (PC: Control-A) to select all of the text and press Command-C (PC: Control-C) to copy it. Then, open the SpeedClinic script in the ExtendScript Toolkit editor, click at the end of the script, press Return (PC: Enter) until you get down to Line 34, and press Command-V (PC: Control-V) to paste the code from the log file.

TURBO BOOST

If you're new to scripting, it's likely you're not using all of the panes you see on the left side of the screen. Feel free to choose Hide Pane from each one's flyout menu to free up some screen space.

STEP FIVE:

Add the following text on a line before the code:

Function addDropShadow() {

Then type a right brace (}) on a line after the Script Listener code pasted in Step Four.

```
File1  SpeedClinic.jtx*
 16    doAction("Gallery Print", "Speed Clinic.atn"); //Run the Action
 17    builder.close();
 18 }
 19
 20 builder.show(); //Show the dialog
 21
 22 function createDialog() {
 23
 24    var dlg = new Window('dialog', 'Gallery Print Script'); //Create a window
 25    dlg.frameLocation = [100, 100];           //This tells where to place the window
 26    dlg.txtName = dlg.add('edittext', undefined, 'Sample Text');   //Add a textbox
 27    dlg.txtName.preferredSize = [200,20];
 28    dlg.btnRun = dlg.add('button', undefined, 'Run');             //Add a button
 29    return dlg;
 30
 31 }
 32
 33 function addDropShadow() {
 34 // ================================================
 35 var id353 = charIDToTypeID( "setd" );
 36    var desc18 = new ActionDescriptor();
 37    var id354 = charIDToTypeID( "null" );
 38       var ref2 = new ActionReference();
 39       var id355 = charIDToTypeID( "Prpr" );
 40       var id356 = charIDToTypeID( "Lefx" );
 41       ref2.putProperty( id355, id356 );
 42       var id357 = charIDToTypeID( "Lyr " );
 43       var id358 = charIDToTypeID( "Ordn" );
 44       var id359 = charIDToTypeID( "Trgt" );
 45       ref2.putEnumerated( id357, id358, id359 );
 46    desc18.putReference( id354, ref2 );
 47    var id360 = charIDToTypeID( "T   " );
 48       var desc19 = new ActionDescriptor();
 49       var id361 = charIDToTypeID( "Scl " );
 50       var id362 = charIDToTypeID( "#Prc" );
 51       desc19.putUnitDouble( id361, id362, 100.000000 );
 52       var id363 = charIDToTypeID( "DrSh" );
 53          var desc20 = new ActionDescriptor();
 54          var id364 = charIDToTypeID( "enab" );
 55          desc20.putBoolean( id364, true );
 56          var id365 = charIDToTypeID( "Md  " );
 57          var id366 = charIDToTypeID( "BlnM" );
```

STEP SIX:

What we've done here is added the code to create a drop shadow on the text layer to the SpeedClinic script. However, we need to tell the script to use this code, so click on Line 15 (just below newTextLayer.text Item.color = textColor;). Press Return (PC: Enter), then add the following on Line 16:

addDropShadow();

```
File1  SpeedClinic.jtx
  1 var builder = createDialog();
  2
  3 builder.btnRun.onClick = function () {
  4    var textColor = new SolidColor;
  5    textColor.rgb.red = 0;
  6    textColor.rgb.green = 0;
  7    textColor.rgb.blue = 0;
  8
  9    var docRef = app.activeDocument;
 10    var newTextLayer = docRef.artLayers.add();
 11    newTextLayer.kind = LayerKind.TEXT;
 12    newTextLayer.textItem.contents = builder.txtName.text;
 13    newTextLayer.textItem.size = 24;     //Modify Font Size if Image is Larger
 14    newTextLayer.textItem.color = textColor;
 15
 16    addDropShadow();
 17
 18    doAction("Gallery Print", "Speed Clinic.atn"); //Run the Action
 19    builder.close();
 20 }
 21
 22 builder.show(); //Show the dialog
 23
 24 function createDialog() {
 25
 26    var dlg = new Window('dialog', 'Gallery Print Script'); //Create a window
 27    dlg.frameLocation = [100, 100];           //This tells where to place the window
 28    dlg.txtName = dlg.add('edittext', undefined, 'Sample Text');   //Add a textbox
 29    dlg.txtName.preferredSize = [200,20];
 30    dlg.btnRun = dlg.add('button', undefined, 'Run');             //Add a button
 31    return dlg;
 32
 33 }
 34
 35 function addDropShadow() {
 36 // ================================================
 37 var id353 = charIDToTypeID( "setd" );
 38    var desc18 = new ActionDescriptor();
 39    var id354 = charIDToTypeID( "null" );
 40       var ref2 = new ActionReference();
 41       var id355 = charIDToTypeID( "Prpr" );
 42       var id356 = charIDToTypeID( "Lefx" );
 43       ref2.putProperty( id355, id356 );
```

TURBO BOOST

Opening the Script Listener log file can take a while as it gets larger. It's good to delete the actual log file often. If Photoshop doesn't see a log file there, it will just create a new one and start over.

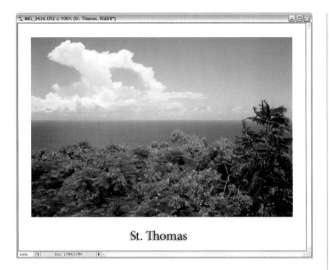

St. Thomas

STEP SEVEN:

That's it. Now you can save the script and run it again on any image and it'll create the gallery style print, but this time the type layer will have a drop shadow layer style on it, as well. I know it sounds simple but trust me, writing that code yourself would not be fun and the Script Listener plug-in really saves a bunch of time.

TURBO BOOST

Visit www.ps-scripts.com for a great forum with discussions relating totally to scripting inside of Photoshop.

UNINSTALLING THE SCRIPT LISTENER

The time will inevitably come when you need to uninstall or stop using the Script Listener. This happened to me when I realized I had to free up some hard disk space on my computer and found that my Script Listener log file grew to over 2 GB (ouch!). Now, since I don't write scripts every day, I just install the Script Listener whenever I need it.

STEP ONE:

First, be sure to close Photoshop. Make sure that a copy of the Script Listener file still exists in Adobe Photoshop CS2's Utilities folder (in the Scripting Guide folder). Delete the ScriptingListener .plugin or ScriptListener.8li file from the folder you installed it in earlier in this chapter (Adobe Photoshop CS2's Automate folder, in the Plug-Ins folder under Adobe Photoshop Only). Once you do this, Script Listener will no longer record what is going on in Photoshop.

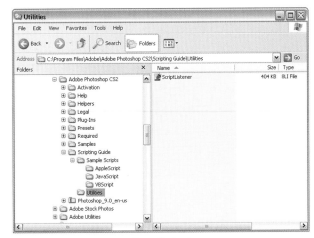

Keep file here

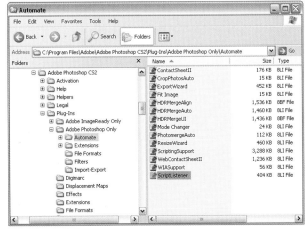

Remove file from here

TURBO BOOST

Stop by www.tranberry.com for some cool scripting-related downloads and some great general Photoshop info. Jeff Tranberry is an engineer for Adobe and he creates some very cool scripts for Photoshop, so it's definitely worth a look.

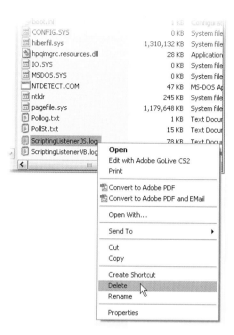

STEP TWO:

Since they are just taking up space now and not actually recording (or listening to) anything, delete the ScriptingListener log file(s) from your Desktop (in Mac OS) or C:\ drive (in Windows).

TURBO BOOST

Photoshop requires your monitor resolution to be set to at least 1024x768. If you set it to anything lower than that, you'll find dialogs and windows will not be fully visible.

CHAPTER 9

GENERAL WORKFLOW SPEED TIPS

SOME FAVORITE SPEED TWEAKS THAT, HONESTLY,
JUST DIDN'T FIT ANYWHERE ELSE

I hesitated naming this chapter the way I did. Workflow is such an overused
word these days but there's no good substitute and, frankly, it's a popular topic.
At any rate, this chapter isn't just about workflow. It's about all of the cool speed-
related tutorials I had that I couldn't fit anywhere else in the book. So I thought
about the one characteristic that they all had in common, and they all related to the
way I work in Photoshop every day. As I result, I lumped them all together into one
chapter, named "General Workflow Speed Tips," because they're things you can do
to change the way you work in Photoshop to get more done each day.

QUICKLY PREVIEWING THE EFFECT OF MULTIPLE FILTERS

When the Filter Gallery was introduced back in Photoshop CS, it didn't make that big of a splash. Many people didn't even know it was there. At first, it was just this huge dialog that took up a lot of space. After I started using it, though, I realized how much time it saved me because now I didn't have to apply 10 different filters separately. Even better, I didn't have to guess how those 10 filters would look once applied. The Filter Gallery lets you build your multiple filter effects visually.

STEP ONE:

Open an image in Photoshop that you'd like to apply multiple filters to. Choose Filter>Sketch>Halftone Pattern. This will open the Filter Gallery dialog with your Half-tone Pattern filter applied to the image. On the left is the preview of what your image will look like after the filter is applied. In the center is a list of all the filters that you can apply in this dialog, listed by category. On the top right are the settings for each filter and on the bottom right is where you'll see the effect layers for each filter you add here. When it comes to the actual filters, nothing has changed—they still have the same settings as they always had. But how you apply them is a lot easier now.

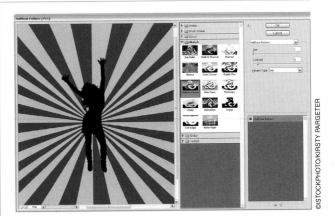

©ISTOCKPHOTO/KIRSTY PARGETER

STEP TWO:

Click the small, right-facing triangle next to any category to expand it and see which filters are available under it. Click once on any other filter to see what it looks like. You'll see the preview change on the left to reflect what your image will look like with that filter, and you'll see the settings for that filter appear on the right side. Go back to Halftone Pattern for this example, though.

Press Command-F (PC: Control-F) to quickly reapply the last filter you ran with the same exact settings.

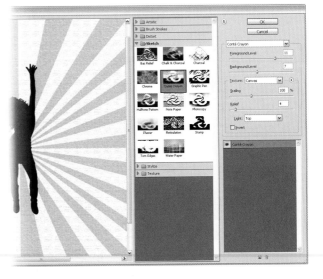

STEP THREE:

Okay, so that's all great but you probably already knew how to apply a filter in Photoshop. However, you can add (or just preview) another filter without ever closing this dialog. At the bottom right of the Filter Gallery dialog, click the New Effect Layer icon to add another filter effect layer. It will be a duplicate of whichever filter is already there.

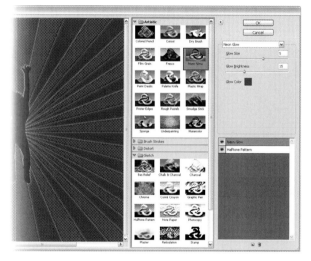

STEP FOUR:

To change the new effect layer to another filter, we're going to expand the Artistic category. Click on Neon Glow. This changes the effect to Neon Glow and displays the settings on the right. You'll also see the effects of adding this filter in the preview area on the left.

STEP FIVE:

Repeat Step Three and Step Four to add as many filters as you'd like. If you want to hide a specific filter from the list to see what the overall image will look like, just click the Eye icon next to the filter effect layer.

TURBO BOOST

Press Command-Option-F (PC: Control-Alt-F) to apply the last used filter but also open the dialog so you can adjust the settings.

STEP SIX:

You can also change the stacking order of the filters, which essentially changes the order in which they're applied, by clicking-and-dragging them up and down in the list just as you would a layer in the Layers palette.

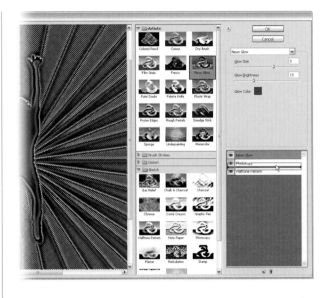

STEP SEVEN:

If you want to delete an effect layer, just click once on it to select it and then click on the Trash icon at the bottom right of the dialog.

TURBO BOOST

You can fade a filter's effects if you choose Edit>Fade, or press Command-Shift-F (PC: Control-Shift-F), immediately after you apply the filter. This also works for adjustments, and even brush strokes and retouching tools.

If you already know how to save your custom settings in a filter, I urge you to read on anyway. This is a very cool technique for adding a vignette to a photo. I never realized the power of being able to save your filter settings until my buddy (and boss, for that matter) Scott Kelby showed me this trick for adding a vignette to your photos using the Lens Correction filter in Photoshop CS2.

SAVING CUSTOM SETTINGS IN YOUR FILTERS

A photo with no vignette

WHAT'S A VIGNETTE?

A vignette is a darkening of the edges around a photo. Sometimes it's caused by a poor-quality lens and sometimes it's caused by certain filters that are added to the lens, or sometimes it's both. Usually, it's something that photographers want to avoid, but at times it really makes a nice special effect to help draw the viewer's attention to a specific area of a photo.

The same photo with a vignette

TURBO BOOST

Now in Photoshop CS2, Windows users aren't limited to the boundaries of the Photoshop window. You can move and expand your image canvas anywhere on the screen, regardless of what size Photoshop's interface is set to.

STEP ONE:

Open any photo that you'd like to add a vignette effect to. I've found this effect works best when you have an area in the center of a photo that you want to draw the viewer's attention to.

©MATT KLOSKOWSKI

STEP TWO:

Choose Filter>Distort>Lens Correction. The Lens Correction dialog will open and you'll see one very annoying thing to start off with—the grid. It totally ruins the photo and just makes it very hard to edit here. So, the first thing I do is turn off the Show Grid checkbox below the image preview.

STEP THREE:

Next, we're going to add the vignette to the photo. (Keep in mind that this isn't neces-sarily the purpose of the Lens Correction filter, but it's a nice trick nonetheless.) Look in, you guessed it, the Vignette section on the right side of the dialog. First, adjust the Amount setting by dragging it to the left. This will start darkening the edges, thus adding a fake vignette to the photo. I find that somewhere around -80 to -90 usually works pretty good here.

TURBO BOOST

If you'd like to apply the previous Lens Correction filter to an image but have modified the settings since then, just choose Previous Correction from the Settings pop-up menu. This will restore the settings you used the last time.

STEP FOUR:

Now, adjust the Midpoint setting right below Amount. This controls the center point of the vignette. Moving the setting to the left brings the darkening effect toward the center (or midpoint) of the photo. Moving this setting to the right pushes the darkening effect more toward the edges of the photo. I usually move this setting to +60 or so, but that may vary depending on your photo.

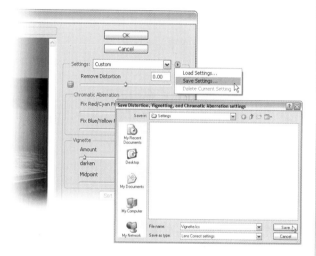

STEP FIVE:

Now that you've adjusted the settings the way you want, you'll need to save them. Click the small, right-facing triangle next to Settings and choose Save Settings from the flyout menu. Enter a name for your custom setting, such as "Vignette," and press Save.

STEP SIX:

If you ever want to automatically use these settings on another photo without having to select them all over again, just open the filter and choose Vignette from the Settings pop-up menu.

TURBO BOOST

To unlock multiple layers at the same time in Photoshop, just target each layer by Control- or Shift-clicking on them. Then choose Layer>Lock Layers and turn off the lock checkbox(es) to unlock all targeted layers.

©MATT KLOSKOWSKI

REDUCING CLUTTER WITH LAYER COMPS

Think of layer comps as a way to keep your Photoshop documents and computer clean, much like you keep your desk clean. When it's clean you tend to know exactly where things are, right? The same holds true for your computer and Photoshop files. If you're working on a project and you save files like Logo1, Logo2, Logo3, Logo1Final, Logo1ReallyFinal, and so forth (come on...you know you do it), in the end it takes a lot of time when you finally do need to find that logo a few months later. Here's a way around that problem.

STEP ONE:

Open or create a Photoshop document with multiple layers. Choose Window>Layer Comps to bring up the Layer Comps palette. The Layer Comps palette helps you create and keep track of your layer comps. You can turn them on or off in the palette to switch between different compositions.

TURBO BOOST

If you want to cycle through a view of only some of your document's layer comps, Command-click (PC: Control-click) on their names in the Layer Comps palette and click the Next and Previous icons at the bottom of the palette.

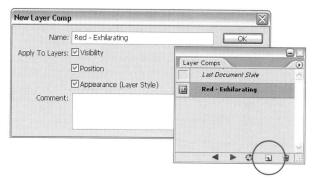

STEP TWO:
In the Layer Comps palette, click the Create New Layer Comp icon at the bottom of the palette to create a new comp based on the current state of layers in the Layers palette. In the New Layer Comp dialog, give the comp a descriptive name (you can even add comments if you'd like) and choose the options you want to apply to the layers (Visibility, Position, and Appearance). Then click OK.

STEP THREE:
Next, try moving around a few layers, or hiding and showing other layers to create another version of the image. Notice how the active Layer Comp icon in the palette returns to the Last Document State at the top. Go ahead and set your document up for the next comp or version of the image you want to save. To record a new comp that shows the changes you've made, click the Create New Layer Comp icon at the bottom of the Layer Comps palette once again. Give it another descriptive name and choose the same options you chose last time. Click OK when you're done.

STEP FOUR:
To view the various layer comps, click the Layer Comp icon next to a selected comp in the palette. To cycle through a view of all the layer comps, just click the Previous and Next icons at the bottom of the Layer Comps palette.

Remember that clicking on the name of the comp only selects it. You'll need to click to the left of a comp to actually apply that comp.

TURBO BOOST

Making changes to a layer comp is easy. Just select the comp and make your changes, then click the Update Layer Comp icon at the bottom of the Layer Comps palette.

SHARING YOUR LAYER COMPS QUICKLY AND EASILY

After I show someone the power of layer comps, the inevitable question arises: How can I share them? They're great for when you're working on your own computer and keeping things neat and tidy, so you don't have several versions of the same file laying around. But what happens when you want to send them off to someone else to look at? There are actually a few options.

STEP ONE:
In Photoshop, open the file that contains the layer comps. Then choose File> Scripts and take note of some of the options there.

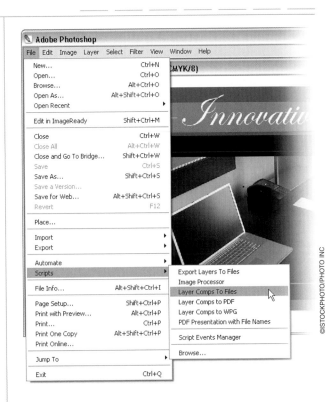

©ISTOCKPHOTO/PHOTO INC

TURBO BOOST

Illustrator CS2 and InDesign CS2 can both recognize and work with layer comps from Photoshop.

Layer Comps To Files dialog

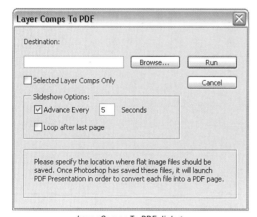

Layer Comps To PDF dialog

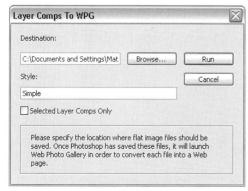

Layer Comps To WPG dialog

OPTION ONE:

The first option you'll see is Layer Comps To Files, which automatically saves each layer comp as an individual file (you can choose between BMP, JPEG, PDF, PSD, Targa, or TIFF).

OPTION TWO:

Next, you'll see Layer Comps To PDF. This is a great option if you want to exchange ideas via PDF. Viewers can quickly switch between your design variations and add their own comments. This means you can communicate with a client about which designs you or they like better and what needs to be changed.

OPTION THREE:

Lastly, you can choose Layer Comps To WPG. WPG is just Photoshop techie speak for Web Photo Gallery. This is a great option if you want to turn all of the layer comps into Web images and get them onto a website quickly so others can see them.

TURBO BOOST

Wondering where Layer Sets went in Photoshop? In an effort to standardize names among the entire Creative Suite, Layer Sets are now called Groups in Photoshop. You can always use the shortcut (Command-G [PC: Control-G]) to create one.

SAVING COMMONLY USED LAYER STYLES

Okay, I have a confession to make here. This tutorial is totally personal. I may be the only person in the world who hates the fact that the Stroke layer style defaults to a bright red color, but I don't care. It's my book and I can write what I want. Now, on the off chance that I'm not the only person in the world that this bothers, or if you have certain settings you really like when using layer styles, read on to see how you can save yourself some time and create a preset of your favorite settings.

STEP ONE:

Create a new Photoshop document (800x600 pixels in width and height) with a black background. Then open a photo and use the Move tool (V) to drag it into this document on top of the black background. Resize it to fit in the center of the canvas, if needed.

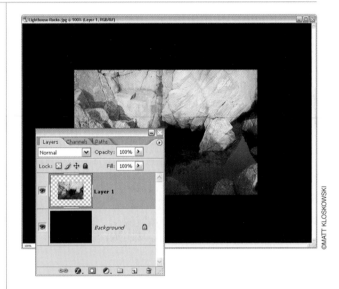

STEP TWO:

I tend to use the Stroke layer style to add a white border around my photos. Let's use a layer style for this. Click the Add a Layer Style icon at the bottom of the Layers palette and select Stroke. Notice how the default color setting is an obnoxious red? On the off chance you don't want to make your photo border red, go ahead and click on it to bring up the Color Picker to change it to white. Also adjust the size setting to your liking and set the Position to Inside so the corners aren't rounded, but don't click OK yet.

TURBO BOOST

You can move layer styles by dragging the Layer Style icon from one layer to another. You can duplicate layer styles by Option-dragging (PC: Alt-dragging) the Layer Style icon from one layer to another.

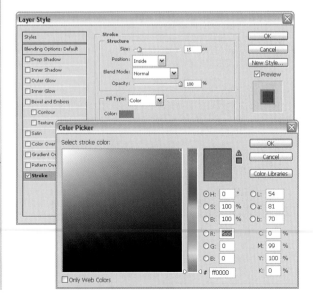

STEP THREE:

When you have the settings the way you like, it's time to save them as a preset so you can use them again without having to change the color, size, and position every time. To do this, just click the New Style button. Give your style a descriptive name and click OK.

STEP FOUR:

To use this layer style, just choose Window>Styles to open the Styles palette. You'll see the newly saved style at the bottom of the palette. Just click on it whenever you want to add it to a photo and you won't have to manually go into the dialog and adjust the settings every time.

©MATT KLOSKOWSKI

TURBO BOOST

The Spot Healing Brush, Healing Brush, and Clone Stamp tool all have a Sample All Layers checkbox in the Options Bar. This allows you to perform all of your retouching on a new blank layer and never modify the original photo.

STRAIGHTENING CROOKED PHOTOS THE CS2 WAY

This tutorial actually came to me while I was writing another tutorial in this book. Earlier in this chapter, I explain how to add a vignette to your photos and save the settings so you don't have to re-create them every time. Well, while I was writing that tutorial I stumbled upon a tool that lets you straighten your photos visually in Photoshop CS2.

STEP ONE:

Open a photo that needs straightening. Unfortunately, I find that I have way too many of them. Okay, maybe not way too many of them, but I do have my fair share (that's why I love shooting digital).

©MATT KLOSKOWSKI

STEP TWO:

Choose Filter>Distort>Lens Correction. The Lens Correction dialog will open. In here, you can repair many lens-related problems that can occur in your photos. This filter is especially helpful if you're not shooting RAW, but it's got a lot of other cool features in it, as well.

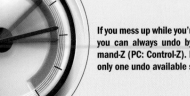

TURBO BOOST

If you mess up while you're in Warp mode, you can always undo by pressing Command-Z (PC: Control-Z). However, there's only one undo available so be careful.

STEP THREE:

The first thing I usually do is turn off the Show Grid checkbox at the bottom of the dialog. Then, along the top-left side of the filter, you'll see some tools. One of these tools happens to be a Straighten tool (I know...I never saw it either!). Using this tool is incredibly simple. First, zoom in to the horizon line. Select the Straighten tool (A) and click-and-drag it along a surface that should be straight. In this example, I'm dragging along the horizon line in the water on the right side of the image.

STEP FOUR:

When you release the mouse button, the filter will automatically straighten the photo. This is the one time where I'll turn the Show Grid checkbox back on just to match up the horizon with the grid lines. There's one small issue, though. You'll see that the filter leaves the edges of the photo looking odd. To fix this you can just increase the Scale setting at the very bottom right of the dialog. Depending on the size and resolution of your photos, and how crooked they are, I find that you can easily get away with a 5–15% increase here. Any more than that and you may want to just press OK and crop the photo outside of the filter.

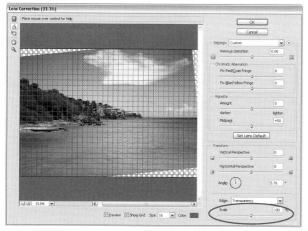

Before adjusting the Scale percentage

After adjusting the Scale percentage

TURBO BOOST

In the Vanishing Point filter, you can quickly zoom in on your cursor when you're creating the perspective grid by pressing-and-holding the X key. Release the key to zoom back out.

ADDING ADJUSTMENT LAYERS QUICKLY

Every time you turn around, writers and trainers are attempting to convey the power of adjustment layers. I'll admit it, I do the same. This isn't a bad thing, though. Adjustment layers are great and really help you create flexible Photoshop documents. However, sometimes it is a pain to remember to add them. Many of us know the keyboard shortcuts for the permanent adjustments, so we often just use them. Well, I've got a trick for you that'll make it easier than ever to add an adjustment layer.

STEP ONE:

Let's use Curves as an example for this tutorial. The default keyboard shortcut for a Curves adjustment is Command-M (PC: Control-M). In order to change this, we'll need to edit the keyboard shortcuts. Choose Edit>Keyboard Shortcuts, or press Command-Option-Shift-K (PC: Control-Alt-Shift-K) and you'll see the Keyboard Shortcuts and Menus dialog appear.

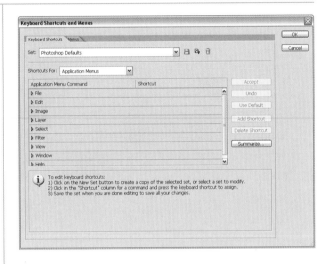

STEP TWO:

First things first. Under Shortcuts For, select Application Menus. Then, click on the right-facing triangle next to the Layer heading to expand it and view the menus underneath. Scroll down until you see New Adjustment Layer.

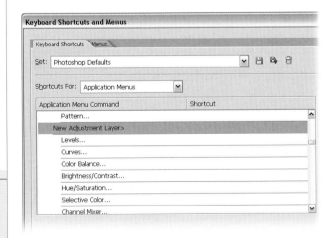

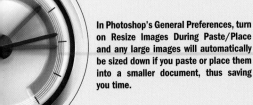

TURBO BOOST

In Photoshop's General Preferences, turn on **Resize Images During Paste/Place** and any large images will automatically be sized down if you paste or place them into a smaller document, thus saving you time.

STEP THREE:

Click on Curves under New Adjustment Layer. You'll see that the entire row gets highlighted. You'll also notice that the option under Shortcut is blank. Just click inside that box and press Command-M (PC: Control-M). When you do this, you'll see a yellow triangle with an exclamation point inside warning you that Photoshop has already assigned this keyboard shortcut somewhere else. It also tells you exactly where. If you choose to keep this change, then you'll be removing the keyboard shortcut from the original location. That's fine here, so go ahead and click Accept. Press OK to close this dialog.

STEP FOUR:

Now, when you're working on a photo that needs a Curves adjustment, just press Command-M (PC: Control-M) and instead of just calling up the Curves adjustment, Photoshop will add a Curves adjustment layer every time. Now that's fast!

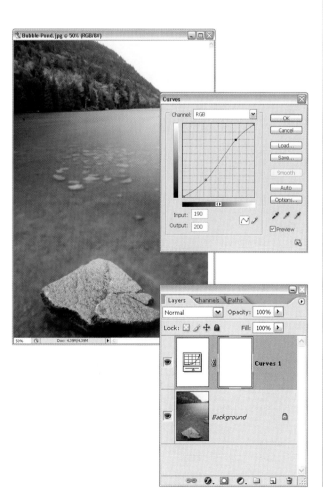

TURBO BOOST

You can group an adjustment layer with another layer by selecting both and pressing Command-G (PC: Control-G). Change the group's Blend mode to Normal and the adjustment layer will only apply to the layer(s) directly below it in the group.

CHAPTER 10

NUTS AND BOLTS

GET UNDER THE HOOD OF PHOTOSHOP AND TWEAK THE SETTINGS TO MAKE IT RUN FASTER

Not many writers would say this, but I have to tell you something—this chapter was really not fun to write. There, I said it. Are you happy? You're probably asking yourself why in the world I would write the chapter in the first place then. Well, think about it. I can give you all the tips and tutorials in the world about working faster in Photoshop, but what good is it if you've got your computer or Photoshop itself set up in a way that will slow you down? So, here we'll take a look at some of the things that nobody wants to talk about—RAM, preferences, scratch disk space, and hard drive space. So, if nobody wants to talk about these things then why am I talking about them? Because they're just as important a factor in working faster in Photoshop as the tips and tutorials that you've read throughout this book.

GETTING THE MOST OUT OF YOUR RAM

There have been a lot of times when I'm working in Photoshop and things really start to slow down. When this happens it usually means it's time to take a look at my RAM and see how much of it is allocated to Photoshop. To get the best results from this tutorial, you should open a few images and go through your normal working process.

STEP ONE:

As you're working in Photoshop, click on the right-facing triangle on the status bar near the bottom left of your document window, just to the right of the current document magnification readout, and choose Show>Efficiency from the pop-up menu. You can use this indicator to determine how Photoshop is doing with the current amount of allocated RAM.

STEP TWO:

If the efficiency indicator goes below 95–100%, then you are accessing the scratch disk which, in turn, will begin to slow Photoshop down. At this point it is still okay, but if your efficiency starts to go below 65–70%, then you may see Photoshop's performance increase if you change your RAM allocation or add more RAM.

TURBO BOOST

When working with preferences in Photoshop, don't forget that Macintosh users can access it from Photoshop>Preferences (Command-K), whereas Windows users access the Preferences dialog from Edit> Preferences (Control-K).

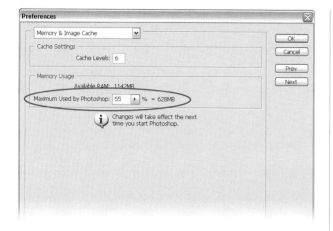

STEP THREE:

If you're still reading, then that means you've realized that changing your RAM allocation or adding more RAM is in order. Unfortunately, this isn't the best place to show you how to add RAM, but I can show you how to allocate more of your installed RAM to Photoshop. First, go to Preferences (under the Photoshop menu on a Mac; under the Edit menu on a PC) and choose Memory & Image Cache. If you've never made changes to this, then the Maximum Used by Photoshop setting should read 70% by default on the Mac and 55% by default in Windows.

STEP FOUR:

Increase the amount of RAM in 5% increments to start (approximately 3% in this case). Click OK to close the preferences.

 Be careful about allocating too much RAM to Photoshop. Don't forget that your operating system still needs RAM, as well, and if you allocate too much to Photoshop then you may still slow things down overall if your operating system is struggling to keep up.

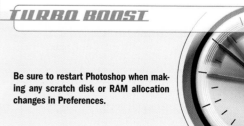

Be sure to restart Photoshop when making any scratch disk or RAM allocation changes in Preferences.

STEP FIVE:

Quit Photoshop and restart. Then open the Activity Monitor on a Mac (go to Hard Drive:Applications:Utilities:Activity Monitor) or the Performance Monitor on a Windows PC (press Control-Alt-Delete to bring up the Task Manager and click on the Performance tab) to see if your Photoshop performance is any better. If you find you still need to increase the amount of allocated RAM, repeat Steps Two through Five, each time increasing the amount of RAM in 5% increments.

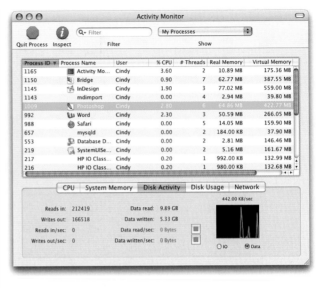

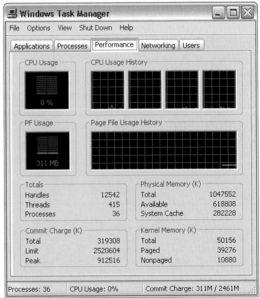

TURBO BOOST

Go to Photoshop CS2's Plug-Ins folder, and in the File Formats folder add a tilde (~) in front of any file types that you don't use to speed up Photoshop's startup time.

I was reading through one of Adobe's support documents one day and saw something about a 3-GB switch in Windows XP that will allow Photoshop to use up to 3 GB of RAM. That was music to my ears, as I've run across plenty of people who commented that, even though they had more RAM, Photoshop could not make use of it. Well, if you're a Windows XP user you may want to try this one.

GETTING PHOTOSHOP IN WINDOWS TO USE MORE RAM

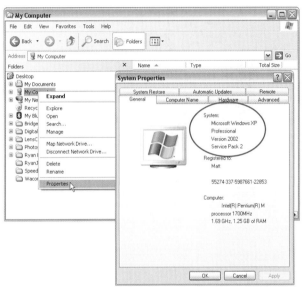

STEP ONE:
First, make sure that you're running Windows XP Service Pack 2. Go to Windows Explorer and right click on My Computer. Choose Properties to display the System Properties dialog. Look on the General tab, under System, to make sure that both Windows XP and Service Pack 2 are listed.

STEP TWO:
Look in the root folder of your C drive. You should see a file named boot.ini. First things first—duplicate this file by clicking on it once and pressing Control-C and then paste it by pressing Control-V. This will ensure that if we do anything bad to the file you'll have a backup.

TURBO BOOST

This one is a favorite of mine. Image Size now has a keyboard shortcut to call its very own. Yep...it's true. Just press Command-Option-I (PC: Control-Alt-I).

STEP THREE:

Now double-click on the boot.ini file. You'll see a bunch of text that probably doesn't make much sense. Update the operating systems line to read:

[operating systems] multi(0)disk(0)rdisk (0)partition(1)\WINDOWS="Microsoft Windows XP Professional" /3GB

Notice the /3GB that has been added to the instance of the OS line. Save this file and restart Windows. Photoshop will now be able to take advantage of 3 gigabytes of RAM.

 The 3-GB switch is a Microsoft switch and may not work with all computers, so you may want to check with Microsoft for instructions before you set the 3-GB switch. You can also search on the Microsoft support page (http://support.microsoft.com) for "3 GB" for information on this switch.

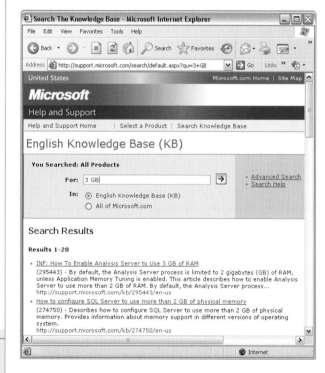

TURBO BOOST

When you switch from Photoshop to another application, by default Photoshop exports clipboard data to the system clipboard for pasting into the other application. If you don't want this to happen, in the General Preferences turn off the checkbox for Export Clipboard.

When you open and work on images, Photoshop first uses your computer's RAM to store information about the image you're currently working on. If Photoshop runs out of its available RAM, it uses your hard drive space to store this information. The hard drive Photoshop writes this information to is called the scratch disk. Photoshop CS2 introduced some changes in the way it manages this memory on your computer.

DETERMINING HOW MUCH SCRATCH DISK YOU NEED

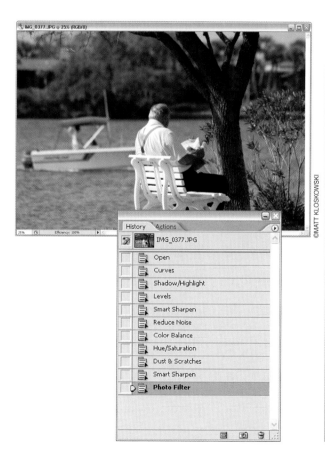

©MATT KLOSKOWSKI

BACKGROUND:

If your scratch disk becomes full, then Photoshop must start to swap out data from your computer's RAM and this can slow things down dramatically or cause them to come to a screeching halt with an out of memory or scratch disk space error message. To avoid this, in the past people used a formula that consisted of taking 3–5 times the size of your average image and specifying that amount as your scratch disk. However, that method no longer provides an accurate estimate of how much scratch disk Photoshop needs. In Photoshop CS2, you can use the states in your History palette to help you determine how much scratch disk space you need.

STEP ONE:

Everything you do in Photoshop that applies a change to the entire image creates a full copy of the image at its original size to store for the History States in the History palette. Think of it this way: if you've got a 1-MB file and you apply the Smart Sharpen filter to the entire photo you'll need 2 MB of scratch disk space. That said, take a look at the History palette for a typical photo that you may be working on and count how many image-wide adjustments you've made.

TURBO BOOST

If you find yourself waiting too long when switching between Photoshop and another application, try choosing Edit> Purge>Clipboard to trash any data on the clipboard and make switching faster.

STEP TWO:

Next, look at the document size in the status bar of your document window. (If you don't see the document size, click on the right-facing triangle on the status bar and choose Show>Document Sizes.) In this example, it's approximately 5 MB. In Step One, I counted 10 image-wide adjustments. To find out how much scratch disk space you'll need, multiply your document size (5 MB) by the number of image-wide changes in the History palette (10) and you should, in this example, come up with 50 MB (5 x 10 = 50). Now, add your original document size to this and you'll have the amount of scratch disk space required to work on this image (50 + 5 = 55 MB).

Now what do you do with that number? Well, let's say the above example didn't use a 5-MB file, but instead used a 100-MB image. Now you'd multiply 100 x 10 and you'd need over 1 GB of scratch disk space. If the hard drive you specify as the scratch disk in Photoshop didn't have that much free space, then you'd run into some problems. In most cases when this happens, people install another hard drive on their computer to use as the scratch disk. If this is the case, then read on.

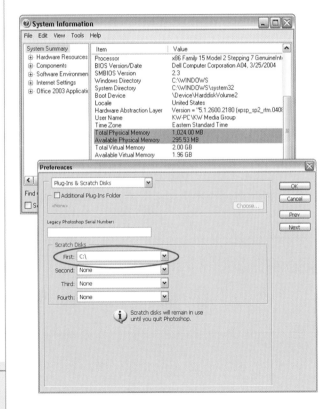

TURBO BOOST

If you want to keep a log of everything you do in Photoshop (and I mean everything) go to Photoshop's General Preferences. At the bottom of the dialog, turn on History Log and save everything you do to a text file.

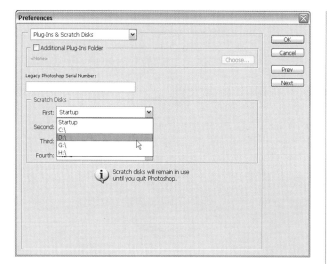

STEP THREE:

Go to Preferences (under the Photoshop menu on a Mac; under the Edit menu on a PC) and choose Plug-Ins & Scratch Disks. This will open the Preferences dialog where you can change the scratch disks that Photoshop will use. To specify or change the primary scratch disk, just choose a hard drive from the First pop-up menu. If you have another hard drive, then this would be the place to choose it. You can also specify a second (and third and fourth) disk, as well, in case the first one becomes full. Do this by changing the choice on each respective pop-up menu from None to a hard drive.

If you've inadvertently turned any warning dialogs off that you still want on, you can always choose Reset All Warning Dialogs in Photoshop's General Preferences.

USING THE PRESET MANAGER TO SPEED UP PHOTOSHOP

On many occasions in years past, I've started Photoshop and sat there for 7 or 8 minutes staring at the startup screen wondering why it's taking so long. I hate to admit it, but I probably even reinstalled Photoshop at one point thinking that would fix this problem. It did, but the problem would always come back again. Finally, I figured out that it had to do with the presets I had loaded into Photoshop. Brushes, patterns, shapes, layer styles, and gradients can all contribute to slow startup and running of Photoshop.

WHAT ARE PRESETS?

If you ever watch the Photoshop startup screen, you may notice that it loads all of your presets (including those you've added yourself) upon startup. These presets include styles, custom shapes, brushes, gradients, and even your fonts. If you're someone who likes to load all of the freebies you can find on the Web (and there are a lot of them), then it's likely you'll see the startup screen for quite a while when Photoshop is launching because it has to load all of the presets you have. If this is the case, then the next steps will show you how you can use the Preset Manager to save and load presets and help Photoshop run faster.

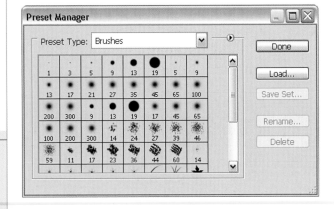

STEP ONE:

In Photoshop, choose Edit>Preset Manager. This dialog is your one-stop shop for managing all of your presets in Photoshop.

TURBO BOOST

If you find that you don't care for Adobe's default file associations, you can change them in Bridge's Preferences under File Type Associations. For example, if you don't use Illustrator you may want to set all EPS files to open in Photoshop.

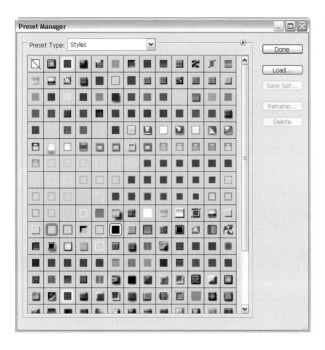

STEP TWO:
Since layer styles are a common culprit and can take up a lot of resources, let's use them as an example. Choose Styles from the Preset Type pop-up menu. As you can see here, I've got a lot of styles loaded and it causes Photoshop to really slow down when it starts up, as well as whenever I work with styles.

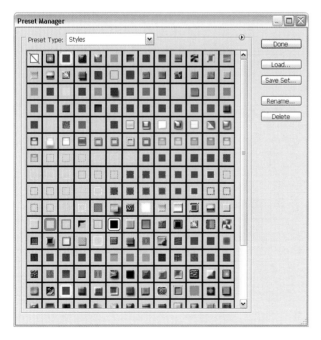

STEP THREE:
First, we need to save the existing styles that are there in case you've added any new ones that you don't want to lose. Press Command-A (PC: Control-A) to select all of the styles in the list. You'll see a dark black outline around them to let you know they're selected. You can always select individual styles to save by clicking on one and Command-clicking (PC: Control-clicking) on any other ones that you want to select.

TURBO BOOST

Press the F key twice and the Tab key once to make your Photoshop image the only thing on the screen. Press F once more and the Tab key again to get back to the regular view.

STEP FOUR:

After you've got the styles you want to save selected, press the Save Set button and you'll see the Save dialog appear. Enter a name for your styles, and press the Save button.

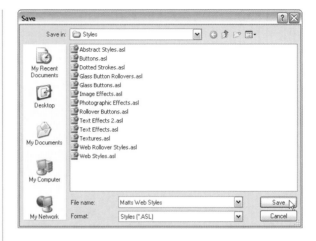

Try not to name your styles "Style Set 1" or something meaningless. You'll find yourself losing control of them quickly if you do this. It helps to categorize the styles like "Aqua Effects" or "Edge Effects," so you can quickly see what type of styles the set contains.

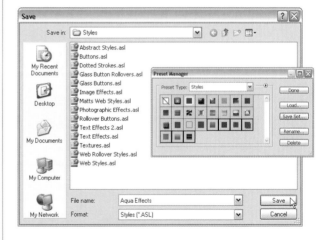

TURBO BOOST

If you quickly want to see two images next to each other in Photoshop, just choose Window>Arrange>Tile Horizontally or Tile Vertically and Photoshop will fit both images nicely in view.

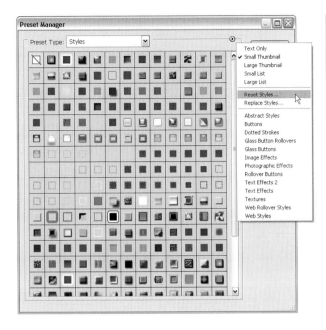

STEP FIVE:

Now that the styles are saved you can go ahead and unload them from Photoshop. Keep in mind that you're not deleting them forever because you just saved them. You just don't always need to have them loaded in Photoshop. To reset the styles, click the small, right-facing triangle to the left of the Done button, and choose Reset Styles from the flyout menu. This will reset your layer styles to the default style presets.

STEP SIX:

Now you can load any additional styles when you need them. To load styles that you've saved or downloaded off the Web, press the Load button on the Preset Manager dialog, and the Load dialog will appear. Find the ASL file you want, press the Load button, and now you'll see them in the Styles list. This means they're loaded into Photoshop and will stay there until you unload them.

TURBO BOOST

A quick way to increase the font size of text is to select the text and press Command-Shift-> (PC: Control-Shift->). Reduce it by pressing Command-Shift-< (PC: Control-Shift-<).

IMPROVE CS2'S PERFORMANCE IF YOU HAVE OVER 1 GB OF RAM

I'm always looking for performance tweaks to help Photoshop run as fast as it can. I thought I'd found them all, but then one day Dave Cross, NAPP's Senior Education and Curriculum Developer (aka Total Photoshop Guru), walked into my office and showed me a really cool trick to make Photoshop CS2 manage memory more efficiently. It really only works if you've got more than 1 GB of RAM, but it works on both a Mac and a PC.

TECHIE BACKGROUND STUFF:

When you work on your images in Photoshop, it breaks your image into sections called tiles. By default, the maximum size of each tile is 132 KB of RAM. However, in CS2 you can increase this tile size by activating the Bigger Tiles plug-in. This means that Photoshop can process large images faster because it won't have to draw as many tiles (there will be fewer overall tiles, since each one is now larger).

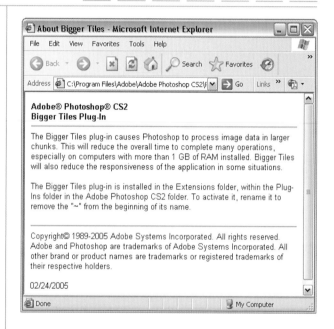

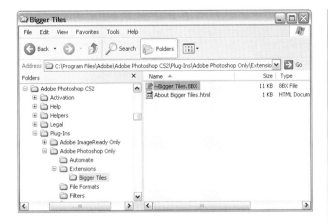

STEP ONE:

First, you'll need to quit Photoshop. Then locate the ~Bigger Tiles plug-in file. On the Mac, it's in Hard Drive:Applications: Adobe Photoshop CS2:Plug-Ins:Adobe Photoshop Only:Extensions:Bigger Tiles. In Windows, it's in C:\Program Files\Adobe\ Adobe Photoshop CS2\Plug-Ins\Adobe Photoshop Only\Extensions\Bigger Tiles.

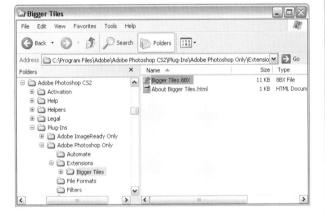

STEP TWO:

Rename the file by removing the tilde (~) from the file name. Go ahead and start Photoshop again. Since Photoshop re-draws more data at a time because each tile is larger, it will process your images faster. I know it sounds a little odd, but Photoshop takes less time to redraw fewer tiles that are larger than it does more tiles that are smaller. Don't ask me why, though, I don't make the rules here.

When using the Hand tool (H), turn on the Scroll All Windows checkbox in the Options Bar to scroll (or pan) all open documents at once.

SETTING YOUR PREFERENCES FOR SPEED

Setting preferences in Photoshop is one of the first things I do every time I sit down at a new computer or install a new version of Photoshop. However, I don't tweak every preference in the Preferences dialog. There are a specific few that I change just because of my personal taste, but there are also a few that I change because it helps Photoshop run faster.

IMAGE CACHE LEVELS:

This one is useful if you find yourself zooming out of your images a lot. Digital photographers will run into this one often because the megapixel count in cameras is getting so high that there's no way to view images at 100% magnification. Cache levels are basically downsampled, low-resolution cached versions of the 100% view that Photoshop can display faster. You can change this option in Photoshop's preferences (under the Photoshop menu on a Mac, or the Edit menu on a PC) by choosing Preferences>Memory & Image Cache. The default is 4 but you can set it as high as 8 if you'd like. If you don't have a lot of RAM (512 MB and under) you may want to set this to 1 or 2. If you've got a lot of RAM (2 GB) you may want to set it at 8 levels. This means Photoshop will give you cached views at 66.67, 50, 33.33, 25, 16.67, 12.5, 8.33, and 6.25%, thus speeding up the amount of time it takes you to zoom in and out of large images.

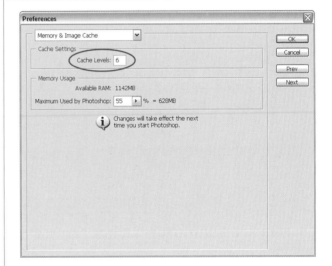

TURBO BOOST

You can reset Photoshop's preferences altogether by holding down Command-Option-Shift (PC: Control-Alt-Shift) when launching Photoshop. Click Yes in the resulting dialog to erase the current Preferences file.

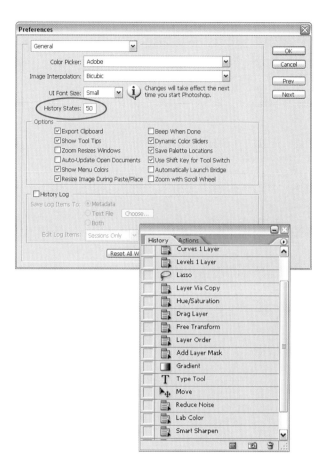

REDUCING THE NUMBER OF HISTORY STATES PHOTOSHOP REMEMBERS:

This one is like walking a tightrope. You have to achieve balance on both sides. On one hand, you may be tempted to bump up the number of History States that Photoshop saves because that gives you more undos. By default, Photoshop lets you undo 20 times which, honestly, isn't enough for me. Maybe I'm just noncommittal, but I change my mind a lot and not having the ability to go back really slows me down. On the other hand, if you increase the number of History States that Photoshop saves to too large a number, then you'll really slow down your editing and image creation in Photoshop. At any rate, the decision is yours and it depends on the way you work, as well as how much RAM you have on your computer. Go to Preferences (under the Photoshop menu on a Mac, or the Edit menu on a PC) and choose General. My suggestion is that if you have at least 1 GB of RAM, then you should set the History States to 50 and Photoshop will now save 50 History States instead of only 20. If you find this slows Photoshop down too much, then try changing to something lower.

ENABLE PIXEL DOUBLING FOR FASTER SCREEN REDRAWS:

Pixel doubling is an option that lets Photoshop redraw your images faster whenever you use tools or commands to move the pixels in the image. Whenever you have an image open and you move the pixels, Photoshop must redraw the entire image. This can take some serious processing power if you're working with a large photo from, say, an

TURBO BOOST

To temporarily turn off a layer mask or vector mask, Shift-click the mask thumbnail in the Layers palette. Then, just click it again to turn it on.

8-megapixel camera. To speed the process up, turn on the Use Pixel Doubling checkbox in the Preferences dialog (under Display & Cursors). Photoshop will temporarily double the size of the pixels in the photo (essentially cutting the resolution of the image in half) for a fast redraw. It doesn't make any permanent changes to the photo and as soon as you're done using the tool, it returns the image to its normal pixel data.

MINIMIZE YOUR PALETTE PREVIEW THUMBNAILS:

Well, this one isn't exactly in Photoshop's Preferences, but it's a preference none-theless. You'll notice that in the Layers, Channels, and Paths palettes there are small thumbnails that preview what is on each layer. You can actually increase or decrease the size of these thumbnails by choosing Palette Options from the palette's flyout menu. Then choose the size of the thumbnail you want. However, the larger the preview, the more resources it takes for Photoshop to redraw them all the time. If you don't have a lot of RAM (512 MB or less) then you may want to keep this one set to the smallest size. I know it's a small tip but hey, we're looking to squeeze every bit of speed out of Photoshop here.

 You'll notice I didn't mention the fact that you can choose None to get rid of your palette previews altogether. That's because while it may speed up Photoshop to have them off, it will slow your work down to a crawl. Trust me, I've tried it, and not being able to see what is on each layer will drive you crazy, as well as slow you down.

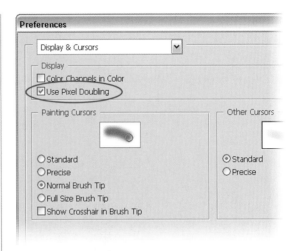

TURBO BOOST

Press the Home key to move to the upper left-hand corner of your image. Press the End key to move to the lower right-hand corner of your image.

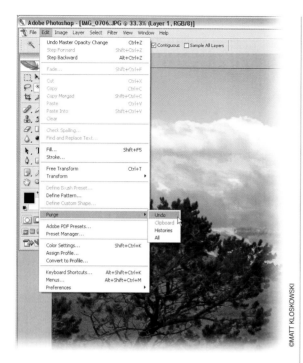

©MATT KLOSKOWSKI

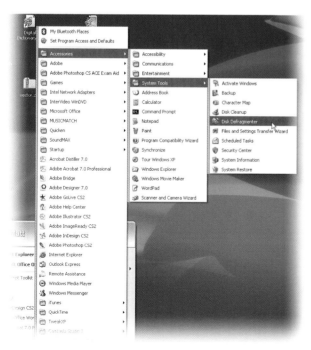

PURGE UNDO, CLIPBOARD, OR HISTORIES:

Purging Undo, Clipboard, and Histories isn't my favorite thing to do mainly because I'm very picky about retaining my ability to undo. After all, that's why the function is there, and you can bet that the one time you purge your undo is going to be the one time you really want to use it. However, if Photoshop is running way too slow, this may come in handy to try to salvage your image and continue working to avoid a system crash.

Undo, Clipboard, and Histories all hold image data. To release RAM, choose Edit>Purge and choose Undo or Clipboard. Choosing Purge>Histories can release RAM or scratch disk, depending on how recent your history data is. To reduce disk space usage, reduce the number of History States available in the General Preferences.

OPTIMIZING AND DEFRAGMENTING HARD DISKS:

Over time, your PC's hard disk can become damaged or fragmented (unavailable in a large contiguous block). If there is not enough contiguous space for the system to save a file, it saves pieces of the file to different locations on the disk. It takes an application longer to read a fragmented file whose pieces are saved in several locations.

To optimize and defragment the hard disk on a PC, use the Disk Defragmenter. Choose Start>Programs>Accessories>System Tools>Disk Defragmenter (Windows 2000) or Start>All Programs> Accessories>System Tools>Disk Defragmenter (Windows XP).

TURBO BOOST

You can reset a tool's settings by Control-clicking (PC: Right-clicking) on the tool icon in the Options Bar (directly under the File menu) and choosing Reset Tool.

CHAPTER 11

BRINGING IT ALL TOGETHER IN THE CREATIVE SUITE

WORK FASTER WHEN YOU'RE MOVING BETWEEN MULTIPLE CREATIVE SUITE PROGRAMS

Well, this is it. You've put up with me through ten chapters (or however many you read before you skipped forward to this one). I thought this would be a great place to cap things off. I've shown you how to use Photoshop to get more work done in less time. Hopefully by this point you've learned that doing things faster in Photoshop isn't just about being faster, but about being smarter, too. Before now, there's been one thing missing, though. Many of you probably own the Creative Suite and don't just use Photoshop, right? Here we'll take a quick look at some of the things that Adobe included in the Creative Suite to help you work faster with all of the CS programs that you own.

SETTING UP THE CREATIVE SUITE WITH THE SAME COLOR MANAGE-MENT SETTINGS

On a typical day, I'll work in Photoshop, Illustrator, and InDesign at one point or another. Many times, I'm saving files from one program and opening them in another. One of the things that always bugged me was color management settings throughout all of the programs. I had to go in and manually set each one of them. If I didn't, I'd risk the colors looking different in each program. When CS2 came out, I was very relieved that they consolidated color management throughout the Suite into one place.

SYNCHRONIZING COLOR MANAGEMENT SETTINGS

STEP ONE:

Open Adobe Bridge. Choose Edit>Creative Suite Color Settings or press Command-Shift-K (PC: Control-Shift-K) to open the Suite Color Settings dialog. By default, the Creative Suite color settings are synchronized as displayed in this dialog.

STEP TWO:

To see more color setting profiles, turn on the Show Expanded List of Color Settings Files checkbox at the bottom of the dialog. To change your color settings for all Creative Suite applications, just click the setting you want in the list, and then click the Apply button.

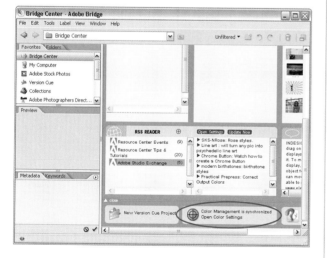

STEP THREE:

The Creative Suite applications are now synchronized using the color setting you specified. You can always check your settings by choosing Edit>Creative Suite Color Settings in Bridge or by choosing Bridge Center in the Favorites palette. You'll see the current synchronization state at the bottom of the window.

TURBO BOOST

To quickly rate an image in Bridge, select the image then press Command-0–5 (PC: Control-0–5). Zero means no rating and pressing any number between 1 and 5 will assign that many stars to the image.

SPECIFYING A SPECIFIC COLOR MANAGEMENT SETTING FOR ONE PROGRAM

STEP ONE:

In Photoshop, choose Edit>Color Settings or press Command-Shift-K (PC: Control-Shift-K). This opens the Color Settings dialog. The first thing you'll see is the same icon you saw in Bridge's Suite Color Settings dialog letting you know that the color settings are synchronized.

STEP TWO:

Change the Settings option to something different than it is now. In my example, I'm changing it from North America General Purpose 2 to North America Prepress 2.

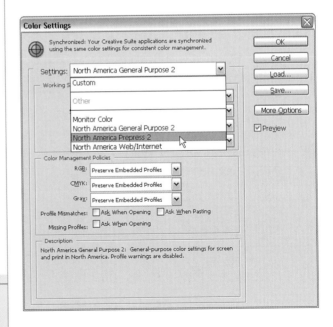

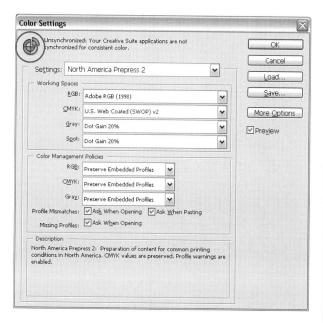

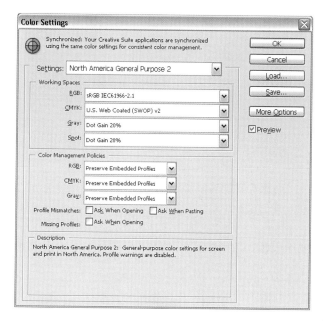

STEP THREE:

As soon as you do this, the icon at the top will change to let you know that the color settings are no longer synchronized for consistent color.

STEP FOUR:

To resynchronize the color settings in the Creative Suite, either go through Photoshop's Color Settings dialog and change the color setting to the setting the rest of the Creative Suite uses or see the previous Synchronizing Color Management Settings tutorial.

When you use Adobe Stock Photos, you can view your downloaded comps by clicking Downloaded Comps in the Favorites palette.

HOW TO MOVE YOUR COLOR SWATCHES FROM PHOTOSHOP TO ILLUSTRATOR OR INDESIGN

One thing that bugged me about working with the same image in Photoshop and Illustrator was my swatches. I'd spend all this time getting my colors in the Swatches palette in Photoshop, only to find that I had to recreate all of the swatches once I was in Illustrator. Thankfully, in CS2 all of the applications can now use a common Swatches palette so you only need to save it once and can use it everywhere.

STEP ONE:

As you're working on an image in Photoshop, open the Swatches palette (Window>Swatches). Click on the Foreground swatch in the Toolbox to bring up the Color Picker, and set your Foreground color to any color that you want to add to the Swatches palette. Then choose New Swatch from the Swatches palette's flyout menu. Give your swatch a name and click OK. Build your Swatches palette this way for any swatches that you want to use in another program, such as Illustrator.

©MATT KLOSKOWSKI

STEP TWO:

You can remove any unwanted swatches from the palette by Control-clicking (PC: Right-clicking) on the swatch and choosing Delete Swatch from the contextual menu. This will clean up your swatches so you only share swatches that you really need.

TURBO BOOST

You can use the Eyedropper tool (I) to sample colors from all areas of your screen (not just an active document). Just click within a document first, and then drag outside of that window with the Eyedropper onto the object you'd like to sample.

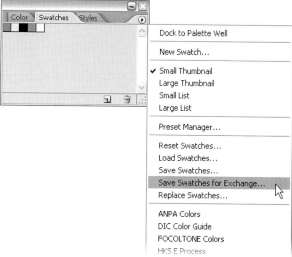

 According to Adobe's help file, you cannot share the following types of swatches between applications: patterns, gradients, and the Registration swatch from Illustrator or InDesign; or book color references, HSB, XYZ, duotone, monitorRGB, opacity, total ink, and webRGB swatches from Photoshop. These types of swatches are automatically excluded when you save swatches for exchange, so be careful. If you don't see a color swatch you saved in one CS2 application when you open another CS2 application, that could be why.

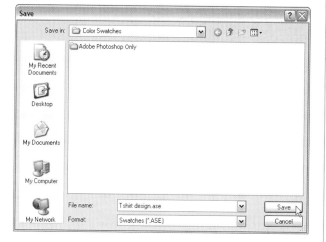

STEP THREE:
When you've got your Swatches palette set up with the colors you want to share, just select Save Swatches for Exchange from the Swatches palette's flyout menu. Choose a location that's easy to remember so you don't have to search for the swatch file later.

TURBO BOOST

Use the Direct Selection tool (A) to drag an element from an InDesign layout to Bridge and it'll turn into a "snippet" and be saved in an INX (InDesign Exchange) format where it can be dragged into any InDesign layout. You can even email snippets to others.

STEP FOUR:

Open Illustrator CS2. In the Swatches palette, from the flyout menu, choose Open Swatch Library, and scroll to the bottom to Other Library. Find the ASE file that you just saved in Step Three, select it, and click Open. That's it! You've now loaded the same exact color swatches you used in Photoshop into Illustrator. How's that for saving time?

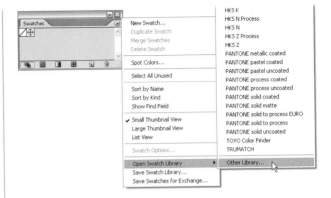

 *One thing that could put a damper on your swatch-sharing bliss is the color settings. The swatches will be exactly the same across all applications as long as the color settings are synchronized. See the first tutorial in this chapter to find out how to do this.*

TURBO BOOST

If you click on an InDesign file in Bridge, look toward the bottom of the Metadata palette. You can actually see what fonts and color swatches the InDesign file uses.

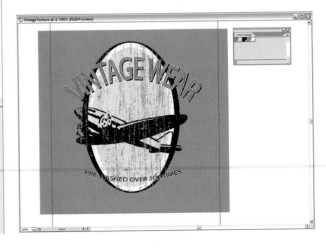

Let's face it—blogs (short for Web logs) are hip. Everybody has one, everybody is reading them, and everybody is talking about them. One problem with blogs is that you have to keep visiting them to see what's new. It's information overload and I know I don't have time to do that. However, Bridge Center (which ships only with the full Creative Suite 2) allows me to view my RSS feeds right inside of Bridge. Now I can just skim the headlines to see what I'm interested in all in one place.

VIEWING YOUR FAVORITE RSS FEEDS IN BRIDGE

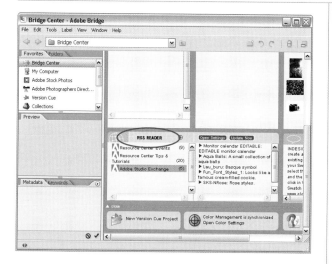

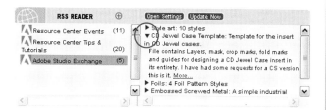

WHAT'S AN RSS FEED?

An RSS feed is essentially a compilation of topics and summaries about those topics. They typically link back to a full webpage of the content or story mentioned in the summary, and they're a quick way to get a glimpse of what's new on a blog. Let's see how to add them to Bridge.

STEP ONE:

Open Bridge and click the Bridge Center icon in the Favorites palette. Near the bottom left, you'll see an area called RSS Reader. This area shows currently subscribed RSS feeds. By default, you're automatically subscribed to several Adobe Resource Center and Studio Exchange feeds.

STEP TWO:

To use the feed, just click on the feed name and you'll see the current topics listed to the right. Click on the small, right-facing triangle in front of each topic to open the feed topic and view a brief overview. You can also click on the underlined More link to launch your Web browser and view this entire feed, as well as see any images that accompany it.

TURBO BOOST

Get more tips and tricks right inside of Bridge Center in the conveniently named Tips and Tricks area in the lower right-hand corner of the window.

STEP THREE:

You may also want to add a feed to the RSS Reader and that's just as easy. First, find a feed that you want to add. There are literally tens of thousands of feeds on the Web. Most news websites have some type of feed that you can subscribe to. To use it, just visit the website and locate the feed (often found by clicking an XML button on the homepage).

STEP FOUR:

Once you've found the feed address, just click the little plus icon next to the RSS Reader title in the Bridge Center window. This will open a small Adobe Bridge dialog where you can type or paste the feed address (or URL). Click OK and your feed will show up in the feed list.

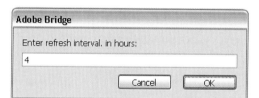

STEP FIVE:

There are also a few more things you can do with the feeds. Click the Open Settings button and set how often (in hours) you want Bridge Center to check the Web and update the feed. You can also manually update the feed by clicking the Update Now button if you don't want to wait for the set time interval.

Choose View>Show>Smart Guides to enable a new feature in Photoshop CS2 that lets you align multiple layers to each other by having them snap into place.

THE FAST WAY TO OPEN ANY IMAGES IN ANY CREATIVE SUITE PROGRAM

I can't count how many times I've double-clicked on an EPS file that I wanted to open in Photoshop and realized that it was opening in Illustrator instead. That's because, by default, EPS files are set to open in Illustrator since that's usually the application people want to use them in. What if you want to change this? Not permanently, but temporarily whenever you want a fast way to open a file that is set to open somewhere else. You'll be happy to know there's an easy way to do this.

STEP ONE:

In Bridge, find a file that you know always opens in Illustrator and click once on the thumbnail to select it.

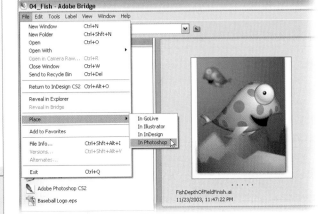

©MATT KLOSKOWSKI

STEP TWO:

Go under the File menu and choose Place. Here, you'll see all four Creative Suite programs (Photoshop, Illustrator, GoLive, and InDesign). Choose whichever program you want to open the file in (in this case, Photoshop) and it'll open there just this time. It won't change the way the file opens permanently, but it will let you quickly open it just this time.

TURBO BOOST

If you look under the Window menu in Photoshop, you'll see various palette names with checkmarks next to them. This means that those palettes are open and visible inside the Photoshop interface.

I had this tutorial in my outline for this book from the beginning because I think it's a cool little feature that goes largely unrecognized. Then, I got hold of Terry White's *Secrets of Adobe Bridge* book. In it, he called this feature the "End of Day button." That's because at the end of the day, you likely have a logo open in Illustrator, some retouched photos in Photoshop, and even a layout in InDesign. At the end of the day, you want to save them all into one group and this feature is how you do it. I thought it was a perfect description.

SAVING FILES AS GROUPS IN BRIDGE CENTER

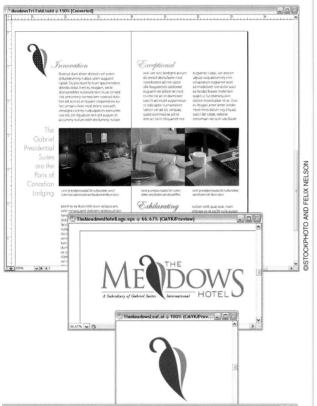

©ISTOCKPHOTO AND FELIX NELSON

STEP ONE:

Let's say you have a logo open in Illustrator, a layout for a brochure open in InDesign, and some photos you're retouching for the brochure open in Photoshop. Basically, these are all files that relate to the same project. You've decided that saving them all into one group would be a huge timesaver, as well as just making your project easier to work on.

Open Bridge Center. You'll see an area at the top left called Saved File Groups. If you haven't saved any file groups as of yet, then the list inside this box will be empty. If you have saved any, then they'll show up here (and you'll probably stop reading this tutorial now because you already know how to do this).

TURBO BOOST

This kind of goes with the previous tip. If you look under the Window menu and you see palette names with a dash next to them, that means the palette is open but it's being obstructed or is behind another palette.

STEP TWO:

To save your files into a group, just click on the Save Open Files into a File Group command. In the dialog that pops up, you'll see exactly how many files from each program will be saved. You'll also need to enter a name for this file group, so give it something descriptive. When you're done, click OK.

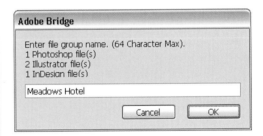

STEP THREE:

Now your files are saved in a group. When you start working on the project again, click on the group that you just saved and all of your files will reopen in their respective applications. How's that for saving time?

TURBO BOOST

Press the Tab key to hide all of your palettes. Press it again to show them. You can also press Shift-Tab to hide all palettes except for the Toolbox, and press it again to show them.

WHERE TO GO FROM HERE

Yep, this is it. I'm done writing the book and you're done reading it. Yeah...I know. You may be one of those people that read through everything in sequence, but I'm guessing you didn't. You probably just skipped right ahead to this part, didn't you? That's okay, it'll be our secret. Anyway, here's a list of resources that I've found very useful to help get things done faster. I hope you enjoy.

FOLDERS ON YOUR OWN COMPUTER:

If you liked the scripting chapter, then you'll need to check out some files that are on your computer. In Photoshop CS2's Scripting Guide folder, you'll see a few PDF scripting guides. One is for Photoshop, one is for JavaScript, one is for AppleScript, and one is for Visual Basic. These will provide you with hours of reading and get you up to speed on scripting and how to start writing your own. There is even a Sample Scripts folder to help you get started.

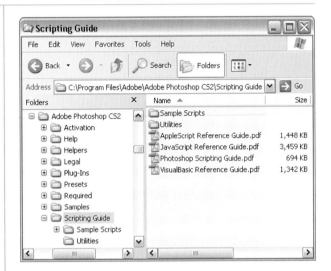

ADOBE STUDIO EXCHANGE:

I have to say, this one should be on the top of your list if you want to work faster. There are thousands of downloads available on this website—everything from actions to scripts to custom presets for Photoshop. If you're looking for something, definitely make this one of your stops. Check it out at http://share.studio.adobe.com.

TURBO BOOST

If you're into scripting in Photoshop or want to learn more about it, check out Adobe's forums page at www.adobe.com/support/forums/main.html. You'll see there is a forum dedicated to Photoshop scripting (and forums for Illustrator and Bridge, as well).

ADOBE PHOTOSHOP CS2 KILLER TIPS PODCAST:

A short and sweet daily podcast by, you guessed it—me! Each weekday, I showcase some cool tip or trick in Photoshop. It only takes a minute or two to watch so you'll be back to work in no time. Check it out in the iTunes Music Store or at www.photoshopkillertips.com.

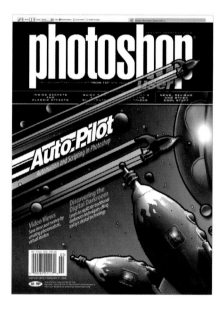

NATIONAL ASSOCIATION OF PHOTOSHOP PROFESSIONALS:

What can I say? I work there, so I have to mention it! Seriously, though, as a NAPP member you get a subscription to *Photoshop User* magazine, which has all of the top Photoshop gurus in the industry writing for it. You also get access to the NAPP members-only website. Now, if you liked this book that means you like me (I hope). If so, as a NAPP member you get access to several new tutorials each week, one of which is by yours truly. Check it out at www.photoshopuser.com.

TURBO BOOST

Don't forget to check out the Samples folder in your Photoshop CS2 folder on your computer's hard drive. It contains a lot of sample images, as well as various pre-built Photoshop and ImageReady droplets ready for you to use.

INDEX

before   *after*

From here to there... effortlessly

Overcome any creative challenge with easy-to-learn techniques you get by joining the National Association of Photoshop Professionals, the most trusted Photoshop® education worldwide.

Join today!

You'll get 8 issues of *Photoshop User* and a bonus DVD!

The "Best of *Photoshop User*: The Eighth Year" DVD. Use code NAPM-1UM for your gift.

Joining NAPP gives you access to:

- Hundreds of handy step-by-step tutorials and downloads
- A subscription to *Photoshop User* magazine
- Online tech support and individual online portfolios
- Discounts on everything from education to computer equipment, travel and more!

A one-year membership is only $99

Corporate, educational and international memberships are available.

 The National Association of Photoshop Professionals

The most complete resource for Adobe® Photoshop® training, education and news worldwide.

800-738-8513 or **www.photoshopuser.com**

Adobe and Photoshop are registered trademarks of Adobe Systems Incorporated

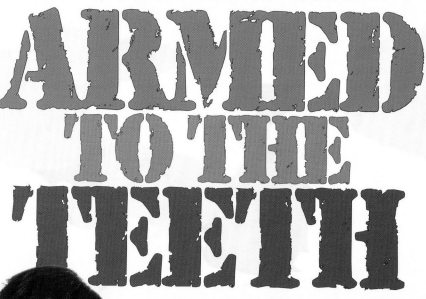

ARMED TO THE 'TEETH

ALL THE AMMUNITION YOU NEED TO BE AN ELITE DESIGNER.

NO CREATIVE PRO CAN AFFORD TO MISS AN ISSUE

- Breakthrough tutorials for Photoshop®, InDesign®, Flash®, Illustrator®, Dreamweaver® and more
- Timesaving design techniques to add to your bag of tricks
- Essential digital photography secrets
- "Tell It Like It Is" product reviews
- Quick wit and award-winning style from the crew that brings you *Photoshop User* magazine

Subscribe today at
www.layersmagazine.com
or call toll-free at **877-622-8632**